THE PIP
FROM SCHOOL
TO PRISON

A True Voyage Through The Prison System

By:

Raymond Melendez

ISBN: 9798690786304

Book Production Melendez Publishing

E-Mail Jrmelpublishing@gmail.com

Printed in the USA

Table of Contents

"FOR THOSE WHO DARE TO CARE"

"Meritocracy banishes the majority of citizens to the margins of their own society, consigning middle class children to lackluster schools and middle class adults to dead end jobs"

– Daniel Markovits

Part One

SCHOOL ROUTE

My Trials and tribulations shed a disturbing light on a familiar Pipeline designed for the unfavorable. Whether your Puerto Rican like me or Black like my allies or boxed in economically there's a trap installed for you. A conveyor belt that shuffles you from the yellow school bus to these steel contraptions called handcuffs. Some Hulu hoop out, but most tunnel further into the Pipeline I'm referring to. My perspective doesn't derive from any higher learning, No PHD don my walls. No clinical jargon spews from my voice box. Just the honest experience of a guy who knows the inner workings of a system who purge the marginalized. Let's delve into the steps that devour my kind. Growing up I was displaced by the custody of wholesome parents and swapped out for the misfits. A mother who was troubled by drugs and a father who bathed in the life style of a pimp. Those routes always lead to one's poisonous outcome. My mother's vice's led her to prison. With my father plunging further into the so called game, an ugly death reached him before natural causes. Leaving a kid to journey a cold world without a road map. With the heads of my household blowing in the win, my Abuela (grandmother) would shoulder the burden of witnessing the emergence of a juvenile delinquent. In a sense, school became my primary guardian. I was particularly fond of gym class and the schools lunch program, especially when they would order take out from one of pizzas most celebrated establishments. Grade School was a comfort of sorts. But with a storyline of a broken home shadowing every bend I made down the school halls that so called comfort would be dismantled. I remember a constant stream of counselor's and guidance counselor's plucking me from one of schools required course's like math or social studies. An awkward interruption would send me rising from my seat with my head down taking each step out of class hauling a boulder of embarrassment due to these frequent disruptions. It wouldn't help that my classmates would rubber neck and belt out investigative sentences like "why do they always take him out of class?" the words that would echo my exit. Now I was being ushered to a smaller classroom where the guidance counselor would probe my thoughts concerning the imprisonment of my mother and the parental disabilities I now faced. Prior to these uncomfortable sessions with the guidance counselor. I was the jovial class clown. Though, I enjoyed the challenge of each school subject and the social bouts of activity we kid's engaged in at recess. The distant cousin of organized sports. It was group building but it was fun. These sessions with the guidance counselor would wane on me. I was reminded of having issues now. School for me became a place that would stress to me that I was riddled with problems that plague the poor. Of course all in hush tones, but I was awake and I was able to feel. Believe me coming to school didn't make me feel good anymore. I was now aware of my low rung social status and how economically challenged my family and I were. School was the last pillar of hope for me and that suddenly fell. When I finally made it to the sixth grade I started attending Raub Middle School in Allentown, PA. I found it odd that there was a police officer stationed in the building. He strolled the hallways toying around with his handcuffs strutting in absolute authority. He once told me he was a one way ticket to juvie hall (detention center) that all I had to do was punch the ticket. A threat he would loosely use to dangle in front of us students. It felt like academics was taking a backseat and security measure's and tactics were disrupting the shaping of young minds. The school faculty patrolled the halls spewing into their walkie talkies, adopting police infused language. They say hind sight is 20/20. I now see with a clear lens. These underfunded school districts encourage the stumbling of the less fortunate. Whether black or brown. We become primed for the goliath system called prison. With the school curriculum withering and security dominating the school's direction. It now seemed like the doorways to the streets opened a bit wider just waiting for me to walk through. The dispairities were alive and menacing for us undervalued kids. Before I ever knew the term the war on drugs that the Regan administration famously coined. Unknowningly, I was boot's on the ground exposed to the fallout of the ongoing war on the poor. What was a kid to do?

Young people want to learn in settings where they aren't surveilled and aggressively policed. I was being stalked by the prison industry constructed by elitist who shuffle the poor from classroom to prison cell. We become victims of a rigged system moving us along this wicked pipeline I speak of. Young girls of color get it the worst. You push a girl out of school because of an educator's version of insubordination. Instead of implementing de-escalation measures. With puberty setting in. Educator's judge her by her rapidly growing body. They no longer see the leader in her. She becomes sexualized and kicked out of school. Desperation sets in. School fails her. Evil embraces her. Prostitution by choice or by force corners her. She takes that yellow school bus from school to prison that was secretly designed for her by the higher ups. We have to wake up an shift the narrative, but without even knowing it, I was making the transition from innocent school student to a strong candidate for juvenile prison. I guess academic stardom wasn't in the cards for me. I was falling victim to the demons who orchestrated the collapse of the poor. At 14 years old as scheduled I made my prison debut. A juvenile detention center at the cedar brook section of Allentown, Pennsylvania. The place was hell. Instead of rehabilitation measures the institution seemed to germanate the hardened criminal in each youth offender sampling the very same facility erected to destroy us. The emotional maze of the place was depressing. However, depression doesn't always mean hiding in the corner. I was front and center, combative as hell. My cry for help was a mother's heartache. Unfortunately, my sobbing sounds went unnoticed. I was circling the drain. I burrowed further into the juvenile system snow balling my stay at the detention center into a long term pause of 15 months. At a placement called North Central Secure Treatment Unit, N.C.S.T.U the place was a prison for kids. Located in Danville, Pennsylvania. Barbed wire hugged the climb resistant fence that would enshrine this gustapo like building that trapped my body. The staff consisted of hillbillies who would mushroom from every corner of Western Pennsylvania who tow around traditional views and values opposing change at any cost.

Pledging loyalty to a system that short circuit people of color, poor and otherwise. The atmosphere of this place was unorthodox for a so called treatment facility who swore by clinical subject matter to shape our undeveloped minds. Instead abusive ways by way of so called restraining techniques smothered and battered our little frail bodies. My first encounter with this brigade of chew spitting high off power corrupt establishment kicked off with Ray Shutt an obnoxious out of shape overly bowlegged, middle aged man with a dramatic kernel sanders mustache to match his outdated tactics when correcting juveniles. I was a kid riddled with trauma inflamed by attitude. This was the guy processing me into this madhouse. After a surplus of questions, I tackled for this man. My irritation reared its head. I kissed my teeth out of frustration. Out of nowhere I was snatched out of my seat and introduced to each furniture fixture discourtesy of the all American body slam. Each pulsating contusion my body was now nursing highlighted the inhumane course of action this place was entrenched in. It's like I stepped into the twilight zone slipping further into the hypnotic swirl the tv show touted until I myself appeared in one of those nightmares. My story being the infamous reformatory for boys , but this was real life and North Central Secure Treatment Unit shared hints of the old reformatory schools for boys that cried foul and was shut down for shady happenings. However, this place was not shutdown. It was actually thriving and feeding off of poor kids. The place mirrored the kids of my neighborhood. The yellow school bus made places like N.C.S.T.U a permanent route. After a while I would just coast along the regular scheduling of the institution. Conforming to the rules of the totalitarian like regime. With me falling in line, a bright spot would reach me from time to time. Some would push back on that thinking. Here's what I mean, aside from the darkness that enveloped the place, a bright spot would occur when the place would host family day for us kids. That would consist of your own section of the yard with your visitors and access to a on-site grill to shell out fast food that would capture your comfort with each bite. But from the group consensus of kids. This should have been a day of shame for me. My family wasn't showing up for me and to make matters worse in the eyes of the other kids. Insult to injury was showcasing my plight. A head count on the basketball court across from the visitors would commence whether you had visitors or not. We all had to line up on the basketball court. After the count you listened with perked ears for your last name to be echoed and once that happened a burst of joy carries you off to your kin. As the line of kids shrinked on the court. I didn't understand why the other kids kept asking me if I was okay. It was no secret there were no visitors coming to make family day a reality for me. I was the last kid to fidget around on the basketball court while my peers hugged and swapped smiles with their family. Eventually, I was waved off the basketball court to meet the staff in the middle of the yard. As soon as I walked up I was astonished at the fact that each guard would actually let their guard down and let their human side surface. In unison they asked me if I was okay. At the time I couldn't resonate with the feelings the staff and other kids communicated to me. I was seeing things different. Back when we were standing around on the basketball court as the group of kids started to downsize. I noticed the mothers of the other kids looking my way as the kids would point in my direction. The concern and nurturing expressions of the mothers registered to me that I was in good hands. Not only was I able to join the festivities of family day, but each location in the yard the families occupied served like some sort of makeshift food dispensary. The fruit salad was colorful and tropical. The burgers and hot dogs sizzled with the distinctive charred stripes from flame bathing on the grill. The pastry section flaked to a crisp. While I was busy constructing a leaning tower of a plate. Smiles and laughter captured the essense of humanity this day. Whether it be the Garcia family or the Williams family love cut through the barracks of the facility and reached me on the yard. That type of bright spot would lose its luster in no time. With the families at the tale end of administering hugs and slowly retreating to their waiting cars in the parking lot. A heap of kids raced towards the fence to belt out one last good bye to their loved ones. I was still hugging this massive plate stuffing my face wafting in the aroma before a drill sergeant like bark, billowed out of the side of this hill billies face. "Count time, count time , everybody on the basketball court now" We were ordered to discard any remaining food and shepherd along the court like sheep. The love fizzled, and the North Korea like regime reappeared. Ray Shutt playing Dictator, channeling his inner Kim Jong Un. I was always wandering when the treatment part of the facility would come swooping in to subdue the aggressive nature canvassing the grounds. I remember this one time a new resident arrived to the facility with this weird limp. It was a mix between a forced bop or a pulled hamstring. I prejudged and thought he was being a little extra maybe some sort of defense mechanism at play. Either way each newbie endured a series of steps before joining the other residents. A vetting process if you will. The last step would be a meeting with the bulk of the residents in the TV room. The newbie would sit in the single hard chair facing the group while giving his name. Where he was from, what led to his incarceration etc. Normal stuff you would think, but to these staff members you had to be perfect. During this introduction stage the pressure would mount. The regime would hurl the most insensitive, dehumanizing remarks towards the kid. Bullying and trolling would best describe the scene. The poking and egging on from the staff only fed the breeding monster festering inside each abusive staff member, patiently waiting for the cue to pounce on its prey. In this case, the newbie blew air out of frustration. A term the staff coined as giving a flat tire. Blatant disrespect in their eyes. A primed and amped up burly hill billy by the name of Mark Beech exploded from the corner like a bull chasing down a matador. The crashing contact was grossly flagrant. The kid was tackled so hard that his left leg that dragged a little to cool earlier on, was now gruesomely flush against his back as he was pinned down you could see his foot peeking over his left shoulder like a ninja's sword would. The freak injury caused a wave of shock that left our jaws to drop in looney toons fashion. And just when you thought you seen it all. The kid gets loose and detaches his leg from his body and throws it across the room. I sat frozen at a loss of words. Come to find out he had a prosthetic leg. Either way the scene unfolded like an episode of Riplieys believe it or not. Disturbingly shocking! This place wasn't providing treatment. If anything, it would foster my disdain for the system. It was a us verse them mentality. So, I continued my destructive path. Loitering on the side of wrong. My next stop along the Pipeline was South Mountain Secure Treatment Unit. Located in South Mountain, Pennsylvania for a violation of juvenile probation. Regarding a conspiracy to robbery. I was a confused kid and this place boasted the exact remedy to curb any of my unlawful ways through so called treatment. This place was nothing like North Central. Back at N.C.S.T.U we retired to our own living quarters at night. The typical kid friendly room. Bunkbed included with a decent thread count of a comforter might I add. Now South Mountain was considered a step higher in security measures. The so called last stop for rebel juveniles, the Shawshank redemption for the adolescence in Pennsylvania. You know, The Morgan Freeman movie. I maybe padding the description a bit with the movie reference, But that doesn't take from the fact that the place was cold. No polite like living quarters. This was my introduction to a cold cell. The sink and toilet was one chrome slab. The visibility in the mirror was like looking at yourself through a car door. The cell's vent seemed to pump out bone-chilling air. The lighting system was unforgivingly bright. It had the creepy hospital ward for the mentally insane vibe and I was smack dab in the middle of this juvenile experiment sponsored by the not so great folks of the commonwealth of Pennsylvania. The police state, my first time joining the other juveniles at this place was in a group session. The chairs were formed into a big circle with the group facilitator at the crown. It kind of reminded me of a scene out of Wes Cravens Dreamcatchers, the Freddy Kruger movie where the institutionally committed juvenile's form the same group session I was currently in to discuss the super powers they hone in their dreams. Minus the super powers. It felt that way. That's the type of shit I used to space off and think about during these groups. My imagination would roam, but again I was introduced to a new regime at S.M.S.T.U though the same pattern of abusive tactics thrived here, but the staff were built much different. The hill Billy body type ceased at the front gate of this place. These guys were hauling around barrels for arms. With the signature gallon of water they trek along the corridors with. It was like a haven for wrestlers with bum knees who transitioned to correctional guards. Funny looking I tell you. I bet a lot of the rage they would storm down on us deduce from a muscle heads choice of nourishment, anabolic steroids. Roid rage was alive at this facility. It was nothing to see one of the overly charged up Randy savage in energy guards show up to my unit spewing wrestle mania like rhetoric. "I will kick your ass up and down this building boy, do you understand me son?" With an open hand playing spear to your face and his middle finger one sixteenth of an inch from your eye lashes, daring you to sneak signs of aggression so they can get their Dwayne "The Rock" Johnson on and whoop your little Ass. But this one time the tide changed. There had to be a big Oh full moon outside the building I couldn't get my eyes on. Because at the moment I was ordered by one of the militants to recover to the front of my cell door with my hands to my side, thumbs touching the seams of my trousers. Military like orders. Without any transgression I did what I was told. My neighbor to the left of my cell was also ordered in front of his cell door. They rarely said anything to this teenager. He was always able to coast without any infractions. Let me tell you why. He was a towering 6 foot 4 inches tall. Football player physique. He looked like he been knocking people out his whole life. This was interesting to see him at his cell door while this boot camp like instructor of a guard scolded him about the teenager thinking he runs the place. I was puzzled to see this guard that was no taller than 5 foot 7 inches, though he was all muscle, rain down the most disrespectful below the belt remarks to this uncommon massive threat. Through my periphery, my left eye was super peaking. Followed by a twitch. My body was alerting to something. Then it happened. The giant man child gave in and picked up the guard as if he was going to body slam him. Instead he threw the helpless agitator into his cell locking the door behind him. The man child viciously pummeled this man. I never heard a man or a human period scream a terrible tone like this. I actually felt bad for the guard. I don't want to see anybody injured the way he was. The place erupted in a full blown riot. I back peddled into my cell locking myself in. The kid was eventually trafficked to the county prison to await adult charges. The facility even dubbed the incident, the March madness incident and I'm not referring to Basketball either. I want to say 2001 or 2002. It's definitely in the history books of the S.M.S.T.U archive. Fact check the place eventually went on a full scale lock down. Medical and counselor appointments were the only movement we got. I was dropping medical slips left and right, surveying the aftermath of the riot. There were kids flat on their stomach with an officer Chauvin like knee to their neck in puddles of urine and excrement. It was crazy and I'm sure unregulated. Eventually things returned to status quo. I forgot to mention the units were labeled in military lingo. Alpha Unit, Bravo Unit, Charlie Unit, and Delta Unit. I was in the Bravo Unit. Your typical drug and robbery cases. Alpha Unit was intake. Charlie Unit was the diabolical block. The sex offender unit. The sex offender unit. I never imagined these type of people existed until I got to South Mountain.

Sometimes they would intermingle the units for group sessions. The back story to Charlie Unit residents would become ear aching. I couldn't stand hearing their stories. And for some reason they all share a distinctive look. Even if you didn't know them or their case you sensed an off-kilter thing about them. Like when you see somebody with down syndrome you can identify the syndrome. No disrespect to people with down syndrome, but with these vile sex offenders I can spot the look a mile away as well. I learned early on to stay clear of the devil's rejects. That may sound harsh but their stories were too much to stomach. I mainly kept to myself. I would Bob and weave institutional issues like a prize fighter. And to never pry into other people's business. I was the kid looking out the observation deck so to speak. Rotating my eyes from left to right. There was never a dull day. This place was the epicenter for bullying 101. It just happens to be that infamous bully of the facility and I paired well on the Basketball court which nourished a decent friendship. Which allowed for me to be a spectator rather than on defense. The other kids would literally squirm when he stomped by, everything about him was roaring. He was another overly sized man child. He was a skyscraper amongst homes. I never agreed with his ways. I just kept my distance when he fed his ego. But there was this one kid that he would harass more than anyone. Khalif was his name. He was from York, PA. The bully was from Pittsburg, PA. The Homewood section. A pretty rough neighborhood. His unwise Philosophy was that nobody from a smaller town can beat him, so it was free rein to walk all over them. Khalif would take all the bully's antics in stride. He would just walk away. He was real humble and just wanted to get home to his family without any setbacks. People teased him that he looked like Steve Urkel from the TV show Family Matters. Though he was tall and lanky with the gumby cut, oversized bifocals. One morning at breakfast line his Steve Urkel similarities rang true when Khalif tapped into his Stephon like alter ego and mustered out enough courage and confidence so when the bully decided on snatching Khalif's honey bun off his breakfast tray. Khalif punched dead center on his chin's button, sending the bully to fall limp on the linoleum. Khalif was shipped out. Days later the bruised bully showed up to a group session with his jaw wired and reputation fractured like his jaw. Weeks later I noticed a liberated feeling amongst the other kids. Down goes Frazier must of been the mindset. The distressed bully no longer held the imposing control over the flock, items he would normally collect on schedule from the kids were no longer springing up. The kids would even verbally spar with this has been. His muffled threats due to the wiring in his mouth and empty cans of ensure he sipped on through a straw amounted to blood in the water. Before you know it another hero emerges during recreation time, specifically a flag football match. This new hopeful spiked the football and ran directly over to the nursing bully who wasn't even in the game due to activity restrictions. And spewed "I'll knock you the fuck out like Khalif did." The kids went nuts over this "You big dummy!" one of the kids in the crowd backing the prospect barked. Once again I back peddled , But this time to a wall that I leaned on with my palms behind my back and my left leg slightly bent against the wall in rest mode. I was an onlooker moments away from the fire works show, that would implode on the one lighting the match BOOM!! Unfortunately for the kid he couldn't carry the momentum left behind by Khalif. He was brutally beat down by the recovering bully and air lifted by helicopter to the nearest emergency room. It was fucked up and a common theme that trails you along the ride through the pipeline I speak of. As I'm literally writing this page for the book, I look up at the TV and see a story on CNN on the effects the Coronavirus will have on poor students. How the rich are constructing private learning pods for their kids. Leaving the low- income students to lag behind. It's obviously dividing the rich and poor further apart. Maintaining the pipeline from school to prison for the less fortunate. We all start off in the throes of the educational tour nament. Your economical background usually sets the tone for where your headed. The prison industry is banking off our left behind communities. Wake up! Eventually I tunneled out of South Mountain Secure Treatment Unit unscathed. Still I was shouldering a chip I couldn't shake loose. The chip grew out of frustration for the lack of attention I was getting from the two institutions that failed me early on, home and school. I was getting my 2pac on feeling like it was me against the world. That fuel would propel me into the throes of corner hustling which would result in a drug charge that landed me in county prison.

Though I was able to secure bail, the gravity of my actions failed to pinch me awake. While on bail I managed to fall further into my funk scoring a negative with a new drug charge. I was back behind the sliding steel doors of the county. This was 2003, Skinny in frame my S dot carter sneakers that just dropped by the Reebok collab with Jay-Z caused a stir on the cell block. In no time I was being shadowed by offers to buy my sneakers. It was clear me and these solicitors weren't cut from the same cloth. Engaging in negotiating about selling my sneakers was addict like. Big Pun used to say "go that way" meaning stay away from me with that nonsense. I was considered a new fish to the county population and at nineteen I wouldn't know the first thing about treading the shark infested murky waters of adult prison. First mistake I made was my way to the shower in flip flops. At least I had the right idea in protecting my feet from the shower floor and its breeding ground for athlete's foot. I thought I was hip, on my way back to my assigned cell from the shower I noticed the unit winding down on noise. I stepped into my cell, reached for my hygiene products and smiled at the fresh aroma of my scent fumigating the cell. I dried my feet and dabbed a sprinkle of baby powder to complete the ritual. I put my prison issues on along with my tube socks and reached for my sneakers only to notice they were gone! The cell was the size of a small bathroom. One scan of the room spelled out a heist in progress. I stormed out of the cell and approached a guy I was fairly okay with and asked to use his sneakers. He sensed my demeanor and intent. He waved me over to his cell and handed me his sneakers. I literally jumped inside the footwear moving swiftly over to the poker table where the overzealous group of bozo's from earlier flagged me down about my sneakers. I was 140lbs soak and wet so I leaned all my focus on the smallest guy at the table who was still about 180lbs and in good shape. But with my luck the biggest and heaviest trouble maker of them all stood up in a wave of hatred exploding into a tirade, "I took em, fuck you gonna do about it?" He was my real- life encounter with debo from Ice Cube's Friday movie. I had to think fast and use brains over brawns. So, in a non-threatening manner I inched closer to him. Assuring him that there was no problem while timing when the correctional guard on the unit would pass by us doing a routine security walk. As soon as the guard passed us. That was my cue, I flung a wild punch at this accomplished bum. I hit him in his face and grabbed onto him and held on for dear life until the guard separated us. I escaped without a scratch. If I didn't do it that way I would've looked like Martin after he fought Tommy "hit man" Hearns.

Part Two

STATE ROUTE

Ultimately, I was convicted of all charges regarding drugs. I was sentenced to one to four years with boot camp recommendation. Which meant I wouldn't see the inside of my designated state prison. Rather, I was sent to the intake section of SCI Camp Hill in Pennsylvania. Awaiting a physical EKG test to make sure I can handle the upbeat tempo of extreme calisthenics. Boot Camp was a seven- month stint. One month in pre -boot camp then six months in Beirut so to speak. Pre- boot camp was the fifty-two fake out. There was nothing boot camp about it. We would get lost in your favorite in house card games. Casino and the staple of any institution, spades. We laughed so hard disregarding any authority sworn in to uphold the rule of thumb at this facility. We moved about in an ungovernable fashion until four in the morning came rolling in. Let me rephrase that, until a metal trash can came rolling in on the twenty ninth day of pre- boot camp "Get the fuck up you maggots." Drill instructors filed into our platoon unit with the wittiest degrading punch lines one can construct to demoralize its subjects. Quehanna boot camp in Pennsylvania was the latest stop on the pipeline. I was assigned to Delta Unit. Diamonds down Delta a phrase coined by the drill instructor who operated the unit. Now this wasn't your typical correctional guard making the transition to drill instructor. This was your life time devout marine, jar head with twenty -five plus years of service under his belt. His name was officer Singer. He was about sixty years old with a barrel of a chest and cannons for arms. He had the body construction of a twenty -eight year old body builder, young and active. His face mirrored an old Clint Eastwood to a T. He was the epitome of the All-American marine. If you keep your eyes open during your trip through the pipeline once in a blue moon you will uncover the likes of people like Singer who wanted whoever he came in contact with to win in the game of life. The tools he used to usher in some sort of discipline in our lives was physical training and DNC (Drill and Cadence) marching. The idea was to turn us into fine -tuned marching machines. No different from your prestigious West point cadets. He was like the coach carter character of boot camp going above and beyond the call of duty for his cadets. He figured the pride each one of us would garner from turning into a cohesive DNC unit would translate into confidence, which could possibly turn into love of self. Which could be the thing that could save your life. I couldn't even be mad at this logic. Love is that powerful.

Around the time I surfaced at the Quehanna boot-camp program it was suffering a hit in its notoriety department the fear factor was gone. The hey days of extreme calisthenics till you flopped like trout in a pool of your own sweat was history. Clinical programming was invading the place. Administration even implemented yard time three times a day like your typical state prison. Officer Singer along with another staple of Quehanna named sergeant Stewart would loath in the changing of the guards. Half the time these disgruntled service men were too busy feuding amongst themselves about how it used to be, to understand what was really going on at the place. You see Quehanna was coed. I was shocked at the evolution as well. We literally were doing time with women. It was nothing to be walking side by side whispering sweet nothings to a pretty boot camper pulling off the Halle Berry in hairdo. Just to glance out at the yard and see a constellation of women lending some glitter to a dark predicament was everything. I was welcoming each new policy the facility would sweep in with open arms. The more relaxed Quehanna got the more involved I got with a Halle. From passing notes, to light kisses, to even feeling warm places. It was grade school like but therapeutic in the highest order. Everybody was in light relationships at the boot camp. Some relationships got messy and would spill over in blatant love triangles. I seen young mothers at the facility eager to get back to her kids lose sight and allow restricted love to sweep her off her feet. Turning seven months at fenceless facility to three years behind a tall wall. Those moments would easily snap me back to reality. I didn't want to see that trend reach my lady friend or double my time for that matter. So, I ceased the foolery and did my best at adopting the doctrine prescribed by singer. Working out and staying fit became my medicine. I enjoyed it so much that I would easily transition to the coveted position of platoon P.T gun. That consisted of being readily available to showcase my cross fit abilities to any foe who challenged Diamonds down Delta to a duel. You see there were other platoons like Alpha Unit, Bravo Unit, and Charlie Unit. Vying to dethrone Delta Unit of its polarizing spot. With a drill instructor like Singer in all his Bill Belichick qualities that would be a tough task to topple the champs. Aside from the women another exciting thing about Quehanna was the games. These were competitions in DNC marching and strong man games. What unit could dial up the most pushups, pull ups and sit ups. The objective was to come in first place to secure the most ribbons to flaunt and dangle off our guide post as we marched throughout the compound in prideful steps. It felt incredible. I had to applaud Singer for his championship ways and installing superior confidence in us. Our platoon quickly went from a bunch of strangers to a full blown family. Graduation was upon us. That was the day we would wave the place goodbye. Our family would be invited to the graduating platoon. We would display our refined marching to our family and also sit in on a few motivating speeches. Capping off the event with food and beverage. Until then we were all smiles when we got to collect our boxes of clothes sent in by our families. Surprisingly, I even got in on the action when my sister Tasha sent the most fashionable attire my way. The platoon even formed a soul train line to strut in our latest garments. You could see the concern operating all through Singers face. He was particularly fond of this group and hoped we applied all the jewels he unloaded on us. We were diamonds in the rough and it was finally our time to shine. Graduation arrived but the celebration was short lived. My unfortunate luck sat me right back down on my ass. Of all things a detainer was lodged against me to resolve the issue it was gonna take up to twenty-four hours. I was in civilian clothes so my civilian attitude emerged. I was beyond distraught. I have seen every last one of my peers file out onto the parking lot to embark on a new frontier. None of my family showed up to my graduation so I wasn't letting anyone down. I was left to steam alone. Nothing was able to quell the vengeance boiling inside me. Singer tried his hand but it was too late. I regressed to the same belief system that walked me into boot camp in the first place. With a day and a half left until the paperwork cleared for me. I used this minor setback as a way to show my ass so to speak, to each authority figure that had a hand in the terrible hazing practices that go on at the institution, despite the detainer I already signed out of the program. So I didn't have to adhere to the same rules or humiliation the other boot campers had to endure. The other drill instructors couldn't subscribe to that way of thinking. They figured if I was still on the premise all is fair in love and war as the proverb goes. With the fresh apparel hugging my core and an air of conceit leading the way. I was now me all over again. I was quick to snap back like a rubber band at any authority figure trying to apply boot camp measures with me. My true colors would radiate like the forbidden rainbow tugging that pot of gold around that I chased in a lawless pursuit. I hovered like a drug dealer waiting to re up. I was finally released. I didn't last longer than 6 months in society. On August 9th 2006 police uncovered 147 grams of cocaine and 87 grams of crack in my residence. I was back chugging along the familiar pipeline.

I want to take a rest stop along the Pipeline for a moment to talk about how the elitist keep the infrastructure of the pipeline fractured proof so it will never collapse. Locking us up is big business. The gatekeepers are under the watchful eye of the pot belly shareholders who run the show. Its designed to make them generational wealth, so that means whatever it takes to line their pockets, which means making it extremely difficult to escape the hooks they pierce you with once arrested. Now that you been charged and you served your time, they send in their henchmen. Probation or Parole, whatever fancy word they choose to cloak them with. Let's not forget the polite women at the collection agency window who represent the cost and fines agency who shake you down no different from the Italian mob. When you miss a payment with this group you don't go sleeping with the fish. Instead you go sleeping in a steel cage sponsored by a county prison. These groups are assembled to keep you around for as long as possible. The goal is to squeeze as much money out of you as they can. They start off by activating probation on you. Your charged monthly to be under their invasion of privacy strategy. If you don't pay it's a violation of probation. Punishable by prison time. Now your being stretched out, this is where the prison industry makes their cut. It gets a lot more hazardous once you make it to prison. They try to keep you for as long as possible with infractions. These incident reports can cost you your release date. Keeping you longer amounts to more dollar signs. The longer your inmate number is active the longer the fat cat elitist puff on their cohiba cigars drumming up plans to erect more prisons. It gets impractical when your asked to submit a home plan from prison and they deny each one for frivolous reasons. Although you submitted a bunch in posh neighborhoods but watch how quick they approve parole rooms in these revolting neighborhoods I speak of. That alone gives you a whiff of the spoilage created by the American justice system. Now back to the regular scheduling of my journey along the muddied pipeline. With a cache of narcotics fingering me as the subject responsible for the poison. I was sentenced to three-and- half calendars in state prison.

Lehigh County charges convict with escape

Updated Jan 03, 2019; Posted Oct 04, 2011

Photo Courtesy Pennsylvania State Police
John Raymond Melendez
An Allentown man walked away Saturday from a community correction center in
Allentown and is being charged with escape, according to a news release.

John Raymond Melendez

, 27, returned Saturday morning to the Hamilton Street center after a granted leave, police said. After refusing to surrender a cell phone, police said, he walked away from the center.

He has not returned as of today, and his whereabouts are unknown.

Melendez was sentenced to up to 10 years in Lehigh County Prison for a 2006 felony drug conviction, according to police. He pleaded guilty to one count of possession with the intent to manufacture or deliver a controlled dangerous substance, according to online court records.

There's a warrant out for the arrest of the 5-foot 10-inch, 200-pound Hispanic male, police report. He has black hair, brown eyes and tattoos on both arms.

Pennsylvania State Police at Bethlehem ask anyone with information to call 610-861-2026.

I had no boot camp recommendation to lighten the sting of my prison sentence. I was now hemmed in by prison watch towers. A high voltage fence that would leave you smoked out of your boots if touched. Barbwire as trenchant as a samurai sword. This was the big house in all its ghastliness. I was now in the choke hold of the state correctional facility of Pine Grove. In Indiana, Pennsylvania. Pine Grove was set up different though. You had the east side and the west side. The unique thing about Pine Grove is that it housed juveniles. Adults on the east side yard and juveniles on the west side yard. Now these weren't your run of the mill juvenile cases. You had your demonic group of killers who reached national attention strolling the prison yard in the same vein of a David Berkowitz, the son of Sam or Eddie Hatchet who dismembered his victims in Jeffrey Dahmer fashion. You also had your gangland murderer's. The place was crawling with juvenile lifers and I don't mean in prison until they turn twenty -one years of age. At the time in Pennsylvania a life sentence for juveniles meant until your natural life expired. As of recent Supreme Court ruling that practice was deemed unconstitutional. Permitting a legion of inmates who were sentenced to life as kids, another shot at a fair sentence. However, the juveniles who would turn eighteen, they would be sent to the adult side with an option for a transfer to any state prison in Pennsylvania. It was a chance to get closer to home, To make it a friendlier commute for visiting families. As for adults it seemed like the classification state prison in Pennsylvania would designate guys from Eastern Pennsylvania to Western Pennsylvania prisons and vice versa. That formula was a sure way to dismantle any existing family support and further lodging the inmate into Favela's of poor decision making. It clearly underscores the rogue elements these institutions activate to see us lose. What's the sense in denying a parole home plan at a relative's home who has a professional job and lives in a middleclass neighborhood with no criminal record. Your parole officer reports back to you that it doesn't fit the criteria. It doesn't matter if you turn in the gold standard parole home plan. They find a reason to deny it. Good people are going to bat for you, but your parole agent shoots it down. Now your back is against the wall. At this point anything will give. You don't want to spend one more day in prison or a halfway house. The pain is suffocating ,but your parole agent tells you about preapproved rooms for rent for state parolees in your city. This becomes music to your ears. You see a shift in parole, you think maybe they want to see us win after all. But the deception rears its head when you notice the building they approved for you is a dilapidated hell house, like a rest haven for an 80's maniac serial killer. The hide out for Jason Voorhees or Michael Myers. Instead your stuck with the mascots of your hardcore drugs. Crack

51

heads and heroin addict serial thieves. The neighborhood is a blatant recruiting ground for drug dealers, addicts, and prostitution. Whatever vice use to speak to you is now feeding your weakness. You have the sense to not even squat at the place. But your parole agent is threatening you with going back to prison because he showed up at two a.m and you were nowhere to be found. The concept of you having a girlfriend and staying a night with her doesn't register to the agent. He now places you on an ankle monitor restricting your movements. The stress is overwhelming so you go for a drink or a puff. Now you got to answer to the dirty urine you created. Your now in the pressure cooker that's baking you alive. You turn into the ginger bread man and run. With a warrant out for your arrest the pipeline embraces you once again. Aside from getting your civil liberties snatched from under your feet. Prison depletes you mentally. Every day is the same exact day like a version of the movie ground hog day starring Bill Murray. By no means was it a happy go lucky environment. Pine Grove state prison would boast a high volume of inmate on inmate violence. You figure with half the population still growing into their brains. These juveniles would emerge as institutional tyrants. The latest prison news feed would entertain and expose massive bloody bouts between foe's. It wasn't odd to see a fellow inmate toe tagged and bagged off a typical fight gone wrong. Till we meet again rest in peace Chevy. It was always crazy to see how when you got sent to prison your thrown in a cell with a complete stranger. You don't know this person from Adam. You two literally live in a small bathroom together. You could be in there for your third DUI and your cellmate could be a deranged murderer. They mix you in with whoever. It sounds funny but the bonding moment is when you have to shit each other down. Meaning when you guys are locked down and your gut starts to bubble and you got to make a bowel movement, you put your makeshift partition up which could be a blanket or a sheet. Your cellmate covers his face and you proceed with your courtesy flushes. In the beginning its degrading, but eventually it's a normal way of life. Once you two get that out the way a bond and a familiarity of each other is formed. You two rarely hang out with each other outside the cell though. Too much of each other is a recipe for conflict. We all already live in a bathroom together and the first thing we see in the morning is each other. So, when the door cracks open were off to the races so to speak, but we do make the best out of it. With a makeshift oven made out of a plastic bucket, we fill it up with water and baking soda or salt to activate the electrical current when we strip the ends of an extension cord to expose the wires that we then fasten paper clips to. You than drop the wires in the water while plugged into the wall. Then line the bucket with a trash bag. Voila! Your inhouse version of the George Forman Grill. Within minutes considering your culinary skills, you could turn your cell into a savory hut, bouncing in spices and smiling off each cheesy bite of Quesadilla you take. You got a TV in your cell so hopefully you channel surf and find a contested NBA game on or a world premiere movie on FX. The atmosphere can serve as a mental escape for a few hours. I also witnessed the other side of two inmates moving in together and it going terribly wrong. In this scenario involving a friend of mine gives you a indication into how precarious these places could be when two cellmates first meet. Usually the guy who has been living in the cell first gives a careful run down of the Do's and Dont's of the cell. Mainly hygiene related. A constant reminder that the disinfectant lies next to the toilet and to always wash your hands after using the bathroom. Also, that we shower every day in the cell. You got some people who believe if they didn't work out or break a sweat they can miss a day. Not in my cell. If you spent the whole day being a human then you took a piss and a dump. Don't be funky wash your ass please. Normally after you two establish that part. A few war stories circulate the cell. It's like showcasing your resume in a sense. If your younger or a bit immature you puff out your chest with your most potent story. My friend let his guard down at an attempt to go silver back and prove his dominance. Here's what I mean, my friend was convicted of a murder as a juvenile and received five to fifteen years. It was almost like a self- defense case. He ended up sharing the case with his new cellmate, going detail for detail ,play by play, even unearthing deep in his legal material the autopsy report revealing points of entry where the bullet made its impact. Little did he know the man that was listening carefully to this queasy story was close friends to the murder victim. The guy was able to tame his emotions through the story. He never told my friend his relation to the victim.

Instead the night concluded. My friend retired to his bottom bunk without a hitch. His new cellmate climbed to the top bunk, I would like to think in a mental fog. With the light's off and my friend sound asleep. I'm guessing the guy put his fog lights on so to speak, and found his way off the bunk. With a heart full of vengeance the guy creates a ligature out of his bed sheet and proceeds to strangle my friend in his sleep, but divine intervention kicks in. Nothing trumps that kind of blessing. That's God's engineering. My buddy is up and fighting for his life. Eventually my friend is too much of a threat to his assailant and he recedes to the back of the cell. A pause in action between the guys carried them both on their feet and alert into the wee hours of the morning without a combative blow. After the morning head count cleared the doors were popped open for breakfast. My friend skips the meal and joins the morning cleaning crew on the unit.

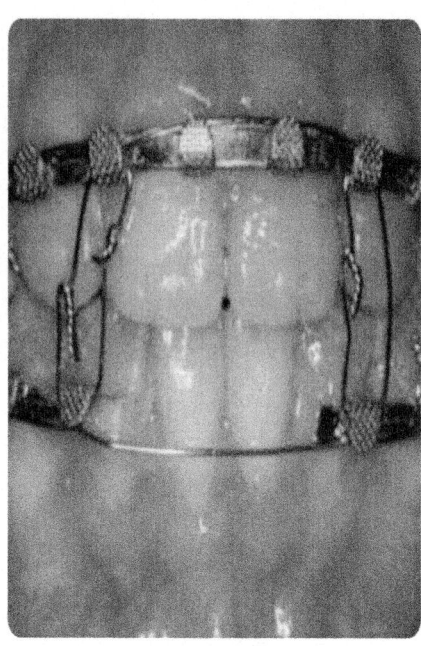

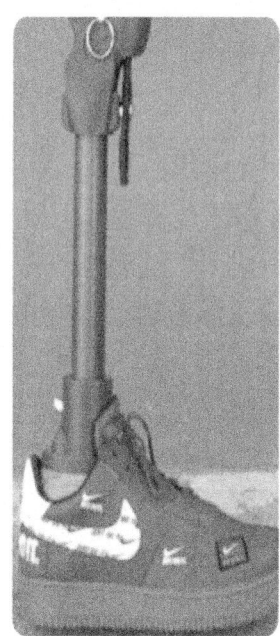

His cellmate stays in the cell as if the incident never happened, after my friend shared the news to his jail house crew. Him and two others armed with mop sticks and detachable metal mop wringers create havoc on this man's skull. Due to his life -threatening injuries the man was air lifted off the compound. My friend and his two cronies were shipped off to the nearest county jail to answer to new charges. Within time the charges for the group of avengers were dismissed. The guy never pressed charges. The victim recovered and was never seen again. That goes to show how you have no idea who you're around during this dangerous ride along the wicked pipeline. That mistake of boasting about an unfortunate situation could have been the death of him. These are the type of incidents that haunt the corridors of prison. It's a haven for bedlam. A fulltime job to maneuver out of harm's way. On top of institutional rules boxing you in. That receptionist you meet when you first come to state prison isn't blowing anything out of proportion when they ask you who do you want your body sent to in the event of your demise. It's actually a fair question giving the extreme violence fanning the prison culture. Another thing about prison that would mess with me to my core, was how some correctional guard's would go out their way to make your stay as desolate as possible. I understand prison is supposed to serve as a deterrent from living a lawless life and the idea is to loathe the experience so much that you don't return. With some of these misguided people they aren't aware or they don't care that America incarcerates its people at an alarming rate. America warehouses more people in prison then any other country in the world. Whatever happen to the land of the free? So, with that discouraging information you would think these guards would be mindful of constricting the inmate further of his rights in the prison. Knowing the lockem down climate America operates on.

These restraints can reach them just as well. There's an old maxim us inmates use regarding the guard's "Do your eight and hit the gate" In so many words just leave us alone. Of course maintain order but don't go looking to abuse your power to swell up in ego because of your inadequateness. I have an uncle who used to be a correctional guard in the county prison. This is before I was lodged in the pipeline myself. I was never able to experience his authority backed by his uniform. I did witness a catastrophic career move that sent him behind the steel curtain of federal prison. Although prison changed his life for good. He now leads his own congregation in ministries doing the lords work. I still wander what type of correctional guard he was during his tenure? Did he abuse his authority in complete disregard for the inmate? Was he a BOA constrictor of a correctional guard squeezing the inmate out of his dignity? But the consummate question would be what was the feeling like going from correctional guard to correctional inmate? The point is this prison thing can reach all. To all authority figures be mindful of the menacing machine prison has become. Help implement prison reform before the machine gets too big and infringes on your rights. It blows my mind that the uneven funding of school districts would be the beginning of my fall from grace. The prelude to the pipeline that sent me from school to prison. Like a lot of us I became the product of my environment, the embodiment of the mantra "Pay for school now or pay for incarceration later." The roaring furnace that is prison spooked me like Macaulay Culkin in Home Alone. As a kid in school I always had an imaginative mind. I would picture myself as a super hero disguised as a student. All along in real life I was being groomed to be a villan. I wanted to be Batman but instead I emerged as Bain. I have more years in prison under me than school years. That's a devastating stat to have.

Sometimes I wish I came into this world with wealthy parents. Attending esteemed schools and getting prepped for success. Instead guys like me are the reason why the lights stay on in these institutions. What if I became institutionalized and I don't even know it. I could subconsciously be more comfortable in prison than in society, you can ask me that question and I will tell you unequivocally that's not the case. I have more work history as a prison orderly than I do in society, that's another disturbing stat. Everything points to me being raised by wolves. The prison industry. Majority of us prisoners are going through the revolving door of incarceration. The booby traps are set to detonate whether we take the wholesome path or not. Parolees become job security for these militarized gunho parole agents. They don't identify as agents of change. When your first released they threaten you with prison if you don't report to them in twenty -four hours. When you meet them their dressed in navy seal attire. In camouflaged sequence, a bullet proof vest, a gun strapped to their thigh. They seem at war. Were no different than the Taliban in their eyes. Wake Up!

My stint at Pine Grove state prison let me in on a disturbing fact. These places are dubbed as the new state hospitals for the insane. Have you noticed the closures of these state hospitals for the mentally insane in your state? The booming construction of state prisons all around you? Maybe not. I can tell you that it's happening at an alarming rate. These state prisons are harboring these suffering patients. Some of these prisoners are out of their minds. Strait jacket, Charlie Manson personalities and the rest are in a zombie state from all the pills they consume. I bet the big pharmaceutical companies have a huge stake in the business of prisons. The pill lines stretch out like the amusement park lines. Administering psychoactive drugs like Thorazine or Seroquel.

I'm sure it's in their best interest to keep these places open for enormous profits. I had a friend that figured if he could stay medicated with psychoactive pills he would be able to escape prison politics. So, he portrayed himself as a mental case to the prison psychiatrist thinking these pills would be Percocet like or something. He got what he asked for and never remained the same. He seemed swollen in the face and body. He went from being overly social to being an extreme introvert mumbling to himself. I draw parallels from the classic movie *Flew over the cookoo's nest* and what they did to Jack Nicholson's character at the end of the movie. That best describes what happen to my friend. That's no hyperbole at all. These places are designed to collapse your psyche. They just didn't expect my friend to give in so easily. He practically walked himself into the office of the evil doctor and like the evil genius they turned my friend into a Frankenstein so to speak. We need to raise awareness and draw attention to the malpractice that's hindering these patients. They need to be in a mental hospital. Not a state prison. The injustice is alive. The most tragic thing I encountered throughout my stay in state prison was with a good friend of mine named Chevy, Chevy wasn't your typical inmate. He was upbeat and smiling most of the time. He had the most ingenious business ideas. While everybody was clutching magazine's with half naked models, he got his fix with motivational content like entrepreneur and Forbes magazine's. He had a logical plan to finally remove any cancerous ambition holding him back. He would beam as he shared each detail of his plans to me. He always reminded me that he wouldn't forget about me, that I would journey with him through the pictures he sends me. It was an earnest gesture. I was just happy he was months away from realizing his goals. A slight skirmish between a foe and I sent me under the prison so to speak. I was now being housed in the restricted housing unit for ninety days of hole time. It was the nature of the beast called prison. It was to be expected. However, I was able to adapt to my surroundings and quickly nabbed a position as the housing unit orderly. Which meant I was barely in my cell. My responsibilities ranged from rolling out trays of prison chow to janitorial duties and passing out fresh linen. It beats being in your cell 24/7. Don't believe the hype of 23 and 1, meaning one hour to come out for recreation and a shower. We came out to shower every three days and maybe the weekends would come haul us to the dog like kennels for a so called stretch. The orderly job was a way to soften the blow of the mental beat down these units excelled in. Eventually, I was able to navigate the torrent waves of stress pulsating through the unit. I even kept an eye out on my fellow inmates boxed in playing hamster, spinning on the wheel so to speak. To my surprise my fellow comrade Chevy joined me in the forbidding ranks of the restricted housing unit. He was three months to the door. He viewed the stay as a search for balance, a chance to equalize before he was off to the races of the real world. He just forgot to figure in he would be sharing a cell with a fellow inmate. This would thwart any plans of the decompressing space Chevy was in search of. A few times he made comments regarding his so called luck in getting stuck with a head case. You know, one of those patients who suffer from mental illness I spoke of earlier. However, these were normal headaches we complained to each other about, prison commentary if you will, but to that extent. As time progressed I would get lost in my orderly detail. I made sure to always check on Chevy. His demeanor spelled out his discomfort with his cellmate. Locked in a bathroom for twenty-four hours a day with a complete stranger whose mentally challenged is quite frankly a challenge. A dispute between the two was inevitable. But that still didn't raise any red flags. Fighting is a way of life in prison. It's a way to cut the tension and restore order. It's a necessary evil. A few bruises that would heal. There was nothing to it. I slid off making my orderly routes. The typical stillness that covered the unit reined supreme. Unfortunately for my friend Chevy, his lifeless body went still after a fight gone wrong between him and his cellmate, he was caught digging in Chevy's neck with a razor after his untimely death. The news was gut wrenching and sad. Chevy was less than three months away from his release date. He was originally in prison for a non-violent drug offense. The pipeline from school to prison swallowed my friend whole. My friend was more than an inmate number who lined the pockets of these fat cats. Without prison reform, sad to say, but stories like Chevy will continue to be a common theme that haunt the prisons of America. I myself wouldn't go unscathed of the Melee reverberating through the prison walls. I guess my number was being called on this particular day. I was in the middle of a battle between the minds, channeling my inner Bobby Fischer in a game of chess. When my opponent rather than playing a silent game, he decided to give a play by play of the game using disrespectful adjectives to describe my failing strategy. A crowd of inmates assembled around us seeking out the next best thing in jail house entertainment due to how dominating my opponents voice rattled the unit. Plus, my irritation with this guy could no longer lie dormant. I snatched a fist full of chess pieces and cocked my arm back no different from a pro pitcher. The pieces stung his face bouncing off the bridge of my rival's nose. We both exploded out of our chairs. Without even realizing it I was still in my slippers instead of sneakers. So, a friend separated us buying me time to race to my cell to put some insurance on my feet. Within minutes like men we arranged a fight in my foe's cell. The guys on the unit carried on as normal to shield us from any exposure from the correctional guards patrolling. Within seconds a barrage of punches started to exchange. In no time our bodies gas tank went empty. Shifting us to resort to wrestling. It was a way to catch our second wind. This strategy proved favorable to my rival. My body didn't get the memo. He slipped some sort of grappling technique on me and put me into a guillotine like choke hold. I couldn't breathe any longer. I was seeing my life flash before my eyes. This man was choking me out. He was going for the kill. My last prayer of a move sent my right middle finger into the man's eye socket in my attempt at gouging his eye ball out of his face. The move spared my life. However, he managed to tilt his head back and bit down on my middle finger like a Twix. The pain shot up like a thermometer stick. Blood oozed out this man's mouth with my finger still wedged between his clenched teeth. I finally kicked him hard enough and pulled my finger out his piranha bite.

Blood was everywhere. You would of thought this was a knife fight from our blood- stained shirts. The fracas of the fight spilled out the cell alerting the authorities. Once the guard barked the order for the whole unit to lock down. That was my cue to run over to my cell as well. Even though I was ordered on the floor. All I was thinking about is the lunch tray I would be missing out on and how I better stick my face head first into my cells locker space that held all my comfort food. I'm sure you're probably thinking how could I think about food after what just transpired. I was actually tapping into my better thinking. I knew an army of guards would burst on the unit extracting me from my cell to ship me to the hole. If your familiar with the hole aside from the idle time. The food rations that they served us were only enough to sustain a Kindergarten. A fight would sit me back there for at least 90 days. This was my only shot to over indulge. I took advantage, as I was woofing down the food. I noticed a bone sticking out my right middle finger. I saw my rival's molar imprints on my finger. I would say the adrenaline surging through me explains why I didn't wail in pain or maybe the fact that a finger is worth losing as opposed to one's life. Eventually the powers that be intervened and protocol was had. Till this day the guys dental records still remain on my finger. The scar is a constant reminder of the finger that saved my life in the Bellator cage of prison.

A large portion of the prison population house men and woman who have no support system. No family or friends rooting for them. There's nobody to champion their goals. Granted, some of these people deserve that cold shoulder. Evil struts behind these walls more so than the noble. However, there's a bunch of honorable men and women stuck behind the wall fully deserted. These people were usually the breadwinners for their family and friends, but now his incarceration limits his philanthropic nature. His reach now falls short. He no longer adds to their bottom line. His influence is now weakened. His name echo's less. His wife or kid's mother was once viewed as lil sis by your so called corner. Their appetite changes course, she's looked at as appealing now. A prize to conquer sexually. Your no longer honored and respected. They never loved you from the beginning. They just loved what you were able to do for them. Your story doesn't even have to resonate with the above betrayal. The abandonment issue alone is enough to trigger radical disdain for your family and friends. The payback mentality grows tumors in you. Your occupied by the get back. Winning by any means necessary is your motto. Eventually you succumb to your poison. Your now diagnosed with prison again. The meat and potatoes of the message is stop leaving your kinfolk for dead when there behind the wall. Your lack of action nurtures the monster inside them. A little support goes a long way. You can inspire hope and change in that person with a little love. It doesn't even have to be in the form of monetary support. A few words of encouragement and some pictures can keep your loved ones balanced and at peace. The worst thing is a vengeful parolee in your neighborhood. It becomes "fuck all of you" everybody gets trampled over just to get his. Trust me. Take heed. Prison is chaos 24/7, 365 days in a year, 366 days in a leap year, but I always manage to escape mentally through the all inspiring prison library. That's my sanctuary. Others may beg to differ and rubuke my perspective as blasphemous. How dare he skip the tabernacle for the library. My version of tapping in to the holy ghost is when I learn something new and informative. Anything thought provoking that can enlighten me is a rush. It sends my heels clicking in the air. According to how the prison library is set up. Whether you have aisles of books or an open wall concept. There lies a treasure chest of wealth in the form of books. These books could be the guiding light and inspiration that molds you into your true form. A light bulb of an idea may beam in your head turning you into the next great 21st century innovator. That's the secret behind some of the greatest minds. A love for thumbing through books turned the gears on between their ears. Who am I to ignore the routes of some of the greats. I religiously dwell in the prison library combing through pages of the most groundbreaking books in hopes that a shift in my mental gears unlock my greatness. Plus, a love for words does it for me. I find it fascinating that the right words can either make or break you. Whether in business or in everyday relationships. So, I figured if I have to be in prison for some time, why not brighten up. I challenge any prisoner to surround themselves around books as opposed to people who will bring you down. I also challenge people who have anyone in prison to send your loved ones some love in the form of a powerful book. Ignite that challenge. Prison can also be a place of body transformation. I have seen frail frames turned chiseled and obese frames melt down to a healthy size. Prison affords you the luxury of time, so we take advantage and sculpt the only temple god gave us. Your probably familiar with the saying prison preserves you, that rings true. We workout religiously and we eat at least three nutritional meals a day. Most importantly were introduced to green vegetables for lunch and dinner. In society fast food places ignore the value of vegetables but in prison we scoop the hell out of some spinach like Popeye the sailor man. In hopes that we to explode in our favorite muscle groups. Plus, the justice system hands out time as if were biblical figures with a couple hundred years of life like Moses or Noah. So, we cling to any routine that will increase our shelf life. Also working out is the best source of medicine for any stress related issues. Fitness is considered a status symbol in the prison yards. Depending on your type of training it can give you the upper hand in any bare- knuckle bouts your confronted with. If your cardio and wind is intact that can be the it factor that can spring you to victory. Of course there's guys who don't do any working out or sports that still manage to get over in a fight. Train so when you bump into one of them you give them an ass whooping of a decade, prompting them to spend sometime in the gym themselves. Plus working out releases feel good endorphins in your body. It's a high your body craves, that's if fitness and training become your thing. It can be a career choice as a personal trainer when you get home from prison. There's a lot of certified personal training programs that will get you started in prison. Im sure the feeling of walking out of prison as a certified personal trainer is a confidence booster. The fitness world is booming. Now you can carve out your own piece of it. Like they say, health is wealth.

While at Pine Grove I was able to secure an outside clearance job working for C.W.P. Community work project. That meant I was off the prison grounds wedged in some community from Monday to Friday 8am to 4pm. We usually did voluntary work for food banks, churches, and highway clean up. We met some amazing people who were very grateful of our services. They would always reward us with boxes of pizza and refreshments but only to get turned down by our C.W.P superiors. Taking food or anything from civilians was strictly prohibited. Us inmates would applaud the gesture though. It wouldn't sit well with some of the people we volunteered for. You would've thought we had union jobs the way they would tap into there Jimmy Hoffa persona's, defending our rights just like Jimmy Hoffa they to would disappear. Of course not in any Cosa Nostra hit. The department of corrections would stop providing them C.W.P assistance. Anybody backing the inmate population would be considered a castaway. As inmates we couldn't sway the vote. Believe it or not, helping these unpretentious people would spark my giving heart. I started to crave the genuine smile these people would compensate us with after each job. Who would of thought giving back would feel so rich. I even vowed to volunteer my services to soup kitchens and old folk homes upon my release. I was also considering adopting a highway back home. That would consist of you and your team keeping your stretch of the highway free of trash. These feelings were foreign, but intoxicating, giving back to your community was the new cool and I wanted in. Unfortunately, my lofty giving never materialized in that manner. I would've loved to have had my own stretch of highway to adopt or volunteering at soup kitchens. Instead I went full blown dealer man like Nino Brown but forgot to pass the turkey's out. Either way I credit the program for inflaming my desire to give back. There's always next time around.

The same way money runs the world, commissary runs our world. With cookies and chips being the hallmark of any grocery aisle, it becomes currency in the big house, bargaining chips if you will. Brand names like Little Debbie's and Tastykakes hold monetary value no different from your favorite dollars and euros. These tooth decaying snacks keep the inhouse economy roaring. There's a price tag for everything. Inmates drive the cost, Uncle Sam is no longer taxing you. You'll be introduced to new Uncles who tax, like the Jose's or the Tyreek's. I'm not speaking in terms of being extorted, that's another story. I'm talking about the jailhouse barbers, the laundry man, the kitchen workers and everybody in between who sustains you. Like Sam Rothstein you keep the palms of your workers greased. This insures a rather different prison stay. Think roach motel versus the Ritz Carlton. Well maybe not that fancy but, you can make it as comfortable as your commissary allows. I met guys in prison who never ate the dining hall food. Instead activate his prison chef to Bobby Flay a dish for him, while waving over the inmate Cake Boss to deliver him a dessert that would rival the Domino's Pizza chocolate lava crunch cake. I don't even mean once in a blue these guys did this every day for years. I also witnessed a few men with zero support turn the institution kitchen into his own farmers market, selling fresh produce like whole onions and peppers, amassing laundry bags of commissary which he would then use to negotiate funds into his inmate account. Even sending money home to pitch in on a small light bill. Those type of actions spoke volumes. Commissary is the reason why plays like that can be made in the bull market of prison. It's also how we skip some of the deplorable meals the institutions try and serve us. Family and friends, if you really care send your kin a few dollars from time to time, to help them escape a bad meal and stimulate some action in the inmate economy. Growing up in the east coast of Pennsylvania in Allentown exposed me to a melting pot of ethnicities early on. You had your Dominicans, Syrians, African Americans, Anglo Saxons and of course my Puerto Rican's. According to your apartment building they lived on each side of you, over top of you, and underneath you. We shared the same schools, city pools and sampled the native cuisine of each group. These were the people you fostered relationships with. When I came to prison I was reminded of a different system of ethics, racism. I started to notice early on if you hung around others outside your race it was frowned upon by your peers, prison politics boxed you into three different groups. Black, Hispanics and Whites. Even if you didn't abide by those politics you were placed in a cell according to your race.

I always viewed it as a Machiavellian move to continue to divide and conquer us. If we stood united it would topple the powers that be. That would be true prison reform. I been to prison with people I grew up with that shared the same belief system as I did regarding other races. Then turnaround and make derogatory statements of other races to his crew just to seem in tune with his group. It seems like the prison factories of America fan the flame of hate for each other. You might of came into the system with a love for all races. The wicked doctrine of prison politics tries to soil what you stand for. The system been in place for so long that it practically runs itself. The higher ups no longer have to step in. The inmate population is brainwashed into doing the dirty work. The goal is to lodge as much hate in you so when you do get released into the free world you keep the old foundation of racism alive and kicking. Dividing the people further. Wake up! Unplug yourself from the scathing Matrix.

The first time I ever played with the idea that I was a prisoner of war was when the History Channel featured a three-part documentary about the Iran Contra affair. How the United States backed the contras with drug proceeds that they got from unloading tons of cocaine in the ghettos of America, led by the head of the national security Oliver North and the head of C.I.A at the time, George Bush Sr. This documentary revealed in so many words that George Bush Sr. was the biggest drug overlord in the world, that the United States bears total responsibility for the drug epidemic that swept America by storm. I was sitting in my prison cell glued to my TV set in shock that this program was airing this documentary like it was nothing. I felt like the government was telling me that "The joke is on you, we traffic metric tons of cocaine because we can , it's a means to an end" Oliver North nor did Bush Sr. go to prison for their crimes, but for a flimsy few kilos of cocaine we get the mandatory minimum of ten years and up. There was also a former D.E.A agent from that era detailing on the program on how he approached then C.I.A director Bush Sr. about how he can prove that the government is behind the mass explosion of drugs ravaging America. How the drug money is collected to fund the contras. He said Bush Sr. the director of the C.I.A cracked a smile and patted the agent on his shoulder and strolled off. The agent went on to say that very exchange sealed what he knew to be true and quit the agency right then and there. It makes you think who are the real criminals? We become scapegoats for the so called war on drugs that they created. Now the marginalized people suffer from their mess. It's like were born to lose. I'm now convinced that I'm a prisoner of war. After two and half years of being cryogenically frozen from society like some sort of demolition man so to speak. I was released onto foreign terrain like characters played by Slyvester Stallion and Wesley snipes.

Part Three

FEDERAL ROUTE

U nfortunately for me I chose the trouble makers path of Simon. This time I fell on the radar of the Drug Enforcement Agency. On November 10, 2016 I was ushered into federal custody at the Lehigh County Prison in Allentown, Pennsylvania. I was being charged with possession with intent to deliver meth and a slew of other narcotics. The meth charge alone would trigger a ten- year mandatory minimum. The federal drug statues for meth are draconian. Fifty grams of meth is ten years in Federal Prison automatically. That means I would fall in the range of no less than ten years to life. Mind you my case didn't involve violence or guns. The sound of ten years was crushing enough. Family and friends poined up enough funds to retain legal counsel to see me get a fair shake. However, when I met my paid attorney I was manipulated into believing I was getting sentenced to ten years in Federal Prison, that I had nothing to worry about because good time and programming would reduce my time to at least six years. It was still a lot of time but a debt to society I was willing to pay for. Through it all my legal counsel abandoned me through each stage of my procedural process. My due process was obstructed, I received two hundred sixty- two months in federal prison. That's twenty -one years and 10 months. A twenty- two -year sentence for a non -violent drug offense. I was devastated at how I was being condemned to a prison sentence more fitting for a murderer. I couldn't believe my prison sentence. When I got back from court my fellow inmates in the county couldn't understand how I was holding it together. Guys were pulling a Jeffrey Epstein for less time hanging by a bed sheet. Naturally I was thinking my lawyer would help me prevail through the appeal process. I later learned I would continue to be deserted by my so called proxy. Within no time I was being transported to a Federal Detention Center in Philadelphia, Pennsylvania. Being from Allentown,

Pennsylvania this would be my next destination along the pipeline of the federal system. The detention center in Philly was a preview of federal time. It mainly housed first time offenders who were fighting their cases or seeing the process through. Guys from my county prison who did FED time already told me to tread lightly in regards to speaking about my case when I got to the building. The ongoing narrative was that there are a host of inmates hopping on each other's cases in hopes to muster up some bargaining chips to offer the government in exchange for a thinner sentence. You also had your prisoners who were back at the detention center from other federal prisons for court hearings. You can sense them a mile away. Depending on their security level you knew who was back from the penitentiary or the medium high federal prisons. Their manners are at an all - time high. It's "excuse me" for everything. They don't cut any lines at the mess hall. They don't walk between tables, they choose the longer route. It's a respect thing. When them lines get blurred lives are lost. The federal system is a different monster from state prison. The FEDS host the 50 states of the United States. Plus places abroad. The B.O.P is practically an international warehouse for criminals. Mexico's own top honcho "Chapo" even dwells at one of these federal infernos. Guys who were sentenced like myself were just waiting to get designated to a home prison so to speak. The process of waiting to find out where your headed to is stressful. You can be carted off anywhere in the country. Midwest, down South, West Coast, even the block of Ice called Alaska.

You find yourself trying to get the attention of your higher powers ear canal in hopes that your prayers keep you closer to home. I was already picking the minds of guys who were back on appeal for any helpful legal advice. Some of these jail house lawyers did legal work in the same vein as a Johnnie Cochran or Jose Baez the super lawyer who helped the terrible Casey Anthony escape a guilty conviction. Some also solicit clients just for a pay day with no direction in sound counsel. They get you by following a template that's already done up. They just insert your name and ID number on the motion and provide you the crisp mailing stamp with a Colgate smile. Mostly you get good people guiding you. I also spent some time in Philly to learn the so called politics of the inmate bureaucrats controlling these haunts. With twenty-two years for a prison term I couldn't accept my plight. I had to log into the law library immediately. I remember during my state prison stint I would hog the screen time of any available law computer to look up big time drug syndicates to learn shrewd ways to heighten my game. Abusing the Lexis Nexis law application. Now I was at the mercy of the law application. Karma is a Bitch! The legal jargon looked

Russian to me. I was having a hard time registering the information. I met guys with thirty to forty years that spoke about getting into everything but the law library. I even heard some say it's a waste of time. I never understood that logic. All we had was time. I also heard people say, "I'ma just wait for one of them laws to pass where they assign you a lawyer that see's where the law applies to your case." I couldn't understand that hopeless energy. I was quick to play Harry Houdini and escape those restraints. Commissary and a fragile MP3 player that they head crack you for keeps you somewhat occupied. They allow you 300 minutes of talk time a month. Even at the detention center you find out quick it's not sufficient enough to maintain healthy relationships. They say the disgraced drug king pin Rayful Edmond was to blame for the 300 minutes of talk time a month. His documentary boasted his unlimited phone calls to his Medellin Partners in Colombia from the prison phones triggering a new indictment and a change in the Bureau of Prisons Policy, regarding the 300 minutes of talk time I'm complaining about. In state prison your confined to people of your state. In the FEDS you mingle with the pulse of the whole country. Its eye opening, a culture shock at times. Us East Coast guys may think the West Coast guys jail strange and the West Coast guys may think we jail strange. It takes getting used to each other. You realize really quick were not so different. I find the slang of different cities entertaining. With some of the most mind -numbing immigration stories of how they entered the United States through shark infested waters in a cheap inner tube or a load of nauseated and puking people crammed like sardines on an eighteen -wheeler cargo for days. Most die from the extreme measures to get into the states. Every gang known to man struts the corridors of these federal facilities. If you pledged a certain allegiance to a certain group in society, more than likely that same group exist on the inside and they know all about you before you land. They'll be waiting on you. If you don't run with anybody, you now do. You find your race or the state you're from. Now that's your new band of brothers. In the beginning you think Huh? Then you realize the environment your now in and it starts to make sense. I never ran with any particular group but being from Pennsylvania I chose my state as my new circle. Plus, I been doing time with Pennsylvania guys since a kid. From Juvenile prisons to state prisons. My fellow inmates were always Philly, Pittsburg, Allentown, Reading, York and Harrisburg. This move would be an easy transition. I made that decision at the detention center. I met a jailhouse lawyer in Philly who overturned his life sentence to thirty years. Then put another motion in that pulverized that thirty into fifteen years. He didn't pass the bar but he knew enough to sway the Judges gavel. That was enough to corral my attention. He shared some encouraging energy with me regarding my cold prison sentence. He told me that the laws are shifting in our favor, that my sentence wouldn't have a leg to stand on if I go and do something about it. He motivated me to jump into my legal work like a cannonball creating my own splash. I felt like my second wind was kicking in. I found hope again. I was now being prepped for my next course of action regarding my legal woes. My lawyer dropped the ball even further. He never filed for my direct appeal. Now that specific window to possibly crawl out was closed shut. The courts give you fourteen days from the day you were sentenced. So, my next vehicle to drive my legal disputes would be a 2255 motion to vacate, set aside, or correct my sentence. My new legal eagle would help me with the road map I should follow when crafting my 2255. He put me in sync with enough legal points to pass on to whoever I chose at my next spot to aide me in my 2255 motion.

I felt confident I would be seeing relief down the road.

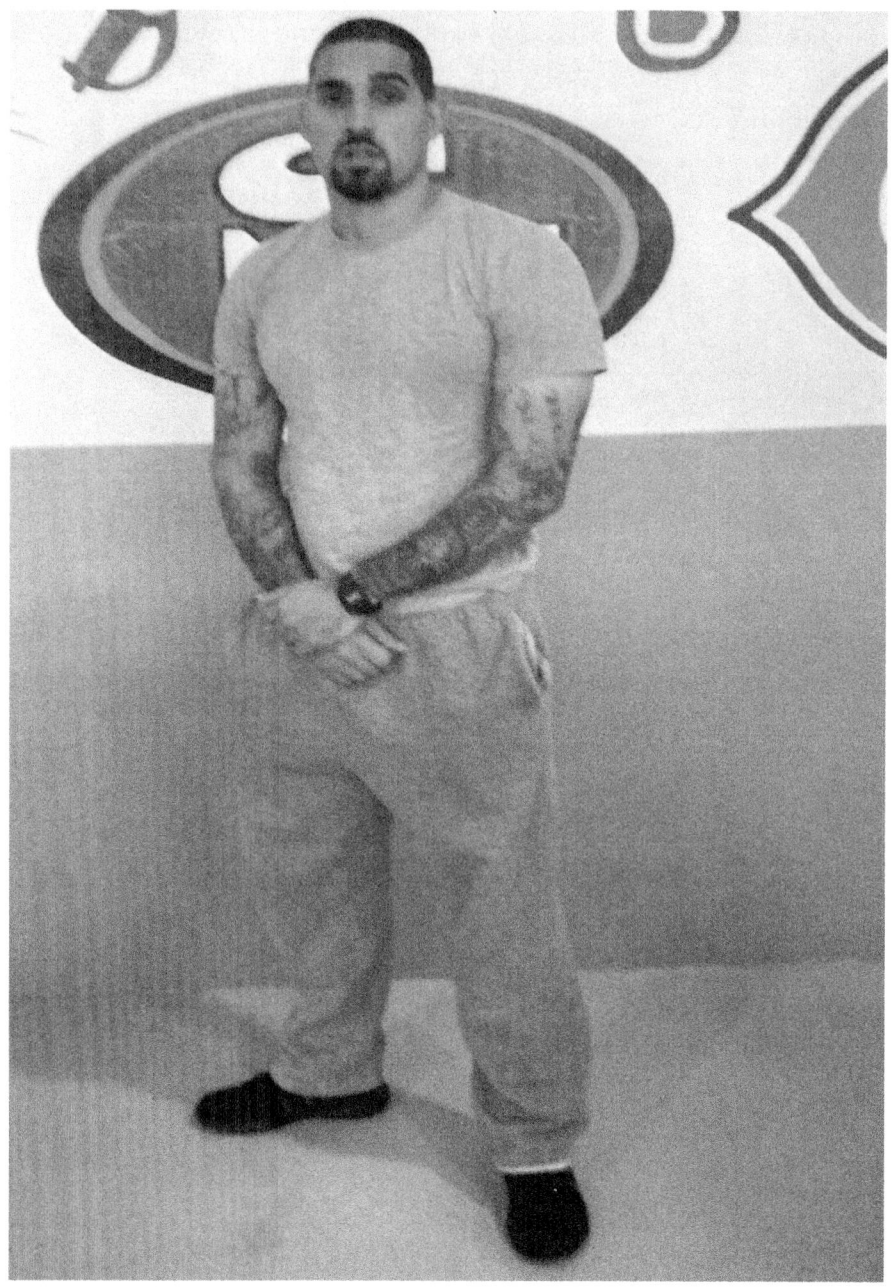

"a moment captured in the inferno of prison"

With a careful review of my legal ambitions behind me until I reached the final Federal building where I would carry out my sentence.

I now emerged as the prisoner I always been courted to be. Whether State time or Federal time, I knew these places in and out. I'm not saying I was comfortable in these places. I just adapted like always. Aside from the back and forth spats about NBA Basketball with my in house counsel. I stuck to a routine of working out with my MP3 player loaded with the soundtrack of my past life. That was enough to turn my sweat sessions into a pro athlete's performance. With enough endorphins flowing through my body I was pacified and relaxed.

I was now able to take in any useful information buzzing through the building like the bottom ticker of a news feed I found out quickly that FDC Philly was touted as the top Federal location for its covetable commissary options. Not only was there a wide selection of perishables that other facilities wouldn't come close to selling. They also sold Parfum like oils in versions of Paco Rabanne and Dior to remind any visitor's that yourself pride is still intact. When I found out what prison would be my last stop through the Pipeline. I was in luck to find someone who was just there that could share to me what items would give me bartering power when I reach my prison. You'll be surprised how these big- ticket items can bridge you to a form of comfort. What little purchasing power I had left I made each store run count. I was now truly equipped to be shipped to my next spot. Lucky for me I wasn't chartering any of the Conair planes the government has in its fleet of transportation. I was partially blessed to stay in Pennsylvania but I wasn't too pleased to learn that I would be sent to a medium-high prison. I was hoping I would be sent to a low. If I had to be in prison I wanted to be where the privliges were in abundance and just like a chameleon I would blend as usual. I finally packed my belongings and was left with a receipt of my property. I boarded the bus in my Hannibal lector like restraints. The seasoned Federal inmates on the bus provided insight on a hold over location we would reach before we were finally dispatched to our final location. The hold over was Metro Detention Center in Brooklyn, New York at MDC Brooklyn. As soon as I reached the unit of this facility you could pick up quick how far of reach the Federal government has. There were a variety of foreigners hugging each corner of the unit. Instead of the typical Basketball or Handball games being played in the pod yard. You had your intense soccer games being played by the Colombians and Jamaicans. This wasn't your typical jailhouse talent. You had your Cristiano Ronaldo types. This one Colombian played professionally in Colombia before he bit the forbidden apple and discovered some innovative ways to send cocaine loads back to the States. The original padrino from his home land Pablo Escobar left a very big shoe to fill. I guess he was tempted. I was glued to these skillful soccer games. The unit even hosted a ping pong table. Instead of doing to much talking and mingling amongst my peers ,I picked up a paddle and resorted to my boys and girls club days. I was Asian like on the table with my serve. Besides working out, that was my favorite pastime at MDC Brooklyn. My cellmate was a decorated brain surgeon prior to bunking up with me in this bathroom of a cell. I guess his morals were corrupted in a white -collar crime. He told me he was headed to a camp FED. The lowest security level in the FEDS. The camps held your debauched politicians and the wolf of wall street type of guys. Even luminaries who decided not to cut Uncle Sam in on their flowing revenue or the Martha Stewarts of the world and their insider trading. You can tell the year my cellmate was giving to serve at a camp wasn't good enough for him. He was in his early sixties, a professional who toasted champagne in Baccarat crystal flute's with high society at elite Gatsby like events. We practically lived in two different worlds. He wanted to know my case through and through. He was so smart in his medical field that common sense and street smarts eluded him. I laid on my top bunk as he laid on his bottom bunk hurling dead giveaway questions of what he truly was up to. "So what are the names of the guys that went down with you?" my misguided cellmate probed. Mind you, my case only involved me, I had no co -defendants. I was blown away by his narrow - minded scheme. I was warned about these slithering serpents early on. It should've never been a surprise to me. Our code of ethics wouldn't align in the slightest way. I' m guessing he also got the message when I told him my supplier was Taylor Swift, he was so out of sync with popular culture that maybe he tried his hand with the name before the government reminded him that Taylor Swift is a pop sensation stupid. His native land is India, so maybe he didn't know the genre. Either way I wasn't the one to score points off of. I ended up moving into another cell with spectacular views of the NYC skyline. At night time I would press my nose to my cell's window enamored by the city lights while listening to music on Hot 97's Funk Flex or Power 105's DJ Self. Gotham city was alive and I felt like one of its villians the cape crusader boxed in with the creepy laugh echoing the asylum. My twenty- two -year sentence would anchor me down into the depths of depression during these sessions at my window. This particular unit I was on you had a bunch of guys who were back from federal prisons to get time back. Instead of everybody moving for self. These guys who were given some light at the end of the tunnel pulled up on guys like me and reminded me that I wasn't going to do anything close to my twenty -two- year sentence. I was told that I came to prison at the right time because the First Step Act was going to reform the laws and help us prisoners currently serving time. At the time I didn't know too much about the First Step Act. These guys were lending me a glimmer of hope. Plus, I started to realize there were guys all around me in worse situations. Some of the guys would've loved to have my sentence. I just wasn't one of them.

My baby boy was living only twenty minutes away from MDC Brooklyn at the time, so I would get a visit every Friday for the six weeks I was there. I hated that he had to see me in prison like that. Especially when he would point at something at the vending machine that he wanted, that I couldn't get up and get for him myself due to prison policy. Despite where I was at my little guy was able to bring a slice of joy to each visit I got with him. He took every chance at showcasing that he was a boy's boy. He played rough and made sure I seen him do his karate kicks. I was losing it inside. I couldn't believe that I left this little carbon copy of me behind. His terrible two's were on full display at the visitation room. He kept throwing his baby bottle at me and thought it was funny that I kept ducking. There was another inmate sitting next to me with his visit across from him like mine were. But he made a costly mistake and waved at my son smiling. My son took it as fair play, when the man looked away I see my son cocking his arm back with a heavy bottle with how full it was. Like in the movies everything went in slow motion as I belted out the deepest, slowest and dragged out "Nooooo!" It was too late the bottle crashed into the man's face. My son thought it was the funniest thing ever. Of course I apologized to the man. He smiled and took it in stride, but I noticed he made sure not to look in my son's direction again. I

was finally packed up and scheduled to head to my final prison.

"my baby boy the bottle flinger at 8months old"

I boarded the bus like routine. Then the news feed on the bus shared one last stop before our final location. United States Penitentiary Canaan.

This federal Penitentiary was considered one of the top violent prisons in the nation. Lucky for us we were just passing by. It's usually a stay of a week or two in a secluded unit. A freezing unit with no way to communicate with your loved ones. No commissary, no hygiene products, no nothing. This place would easily trigger my depression once again. I sat in my cell stone faced and at a loss of words. "What the fuck is happening to me?" Would echo in my mind. Luckily for me I only spent between four or five hours at the prison before I was alerted that I was boarding the bus to my final location. I finally arrived to my next miserable habitat in North Western Pennsylvania. This medium high federal inferno would host me until some good news found me or my sentence was completed. The prison complex fit the architectural structure of my previous stints at juvenile and state prisons. The large slabs of concrete steel and rows of swirling barbed wire that capped the fence so violently became a common landscape to me. No different from shrubs and planted flowers. Sad to say, but I knew these wretched places all to well. I knew the identity and angle of each inmate I came in contact with after only a few conversations. Being in and out of prison since a young teen I've come in contact with all walks of life concerning the condemned. Again, this place was no different. The fake personas and tough exteriors were all cries for help. Like a sort of defense mechanism. I couldn't help but grin to myself when an actor would climb on stage so to speak. I guess I was an observer at heart, jotting down mental notes of my surroundings. I would link with my fellow Pennsylvanians in no time. Your state and city was your crew outside of any gang activity. You now had to be mindful of forty-nine other States and whatever factions of crews derived from them places. So you and your State would go through the bonding process after you been vetted of all documents regarding court dates to get a sense of who you really are. A background check in so many words. If you make it through that process its crew love to an extent. Now your prison stay begins. It's nothing like State prison as far as the comfort you get over there. The number one complaint besides the time you got was the fact that we had no TV's in our cell. That luxury didn't exist in the FEDS unless you were an inmate at the ADX Super Max in Florence, Colorado so I heard. You wouldn't want to be underground for no damn TV.

The so called day rooms on each unit is where we viewed the idiot box. You had to plug your head phones into your MP3 player or Radio to tune into your favorite guilty pleasure.

There's about six TV's on each unit. You got your sports TV, The Spanish TV, the movie TV, according to the unit your on. That TV belongs to a certain party. Everybody respects the rules that are in place. Were assigned two hard plastic chairs for each cell. You place your chair in front of the TV according to how long you been on the unit or where your group sits. Your chair is considered prime Real Estate if you have a spot in front of the TV. There is about five or six computers on each unit to message family and friends from. Some of you on the outside may be familiar with the Corrilink system I'm speaking of. It's pretty primitive considering the state prisons in Pennsylvania allow inmates electronic tablets to reach out to your folks and a bunch of other amenities to download music, games and movies. The FEDS lag behind in the entertainment factor. I was also surprised to hear the feds don't allow conjugal visits despite it being a federal funded program. I couldn't understand how federal inmates were excused from that type of warmth. Of course the FEDS had some perks of its own. These federal buildings would host top notch chef's in the form of inmates. What some of these guys were able to do with a microwave was unbelievable. The creativity and artistry of each dish would promote wide smiles and swollen bellies. It also helps that each unit has an ice machine. A chilled beverage to go with your entrée was everything. I'm not a soda guy but it was a fulltime job to resist an orange crush to help wash down some fried rice. I swear these eventful cook offs involved creativity that should be must see TV for one of them *Parts Unknown* by the late Anthony Bourdain. Society would have tuned in, in droves. The indoor and outdoor recreation area is where us inmates would loiter for big portions of the day. The prison yard unveiled enough space to find your corner to greet you and your comrades with medicine balls in toll. If you plan on having that type of rec or you can head into the indoor excercise room where it's no different from your brick and mortar box gyms, minus the dumb bells. There's three fifty -inch flat screen TV's stretched along the walls to keep your sports fix in comfortable views. In the same room there's a door that leads to the music room where live acts perform using studio quality equipment. It's a place the guys go to escape mentally. Back out the door wedged in a corner are tables where card games percolate like casino tables where dice games echo the allure of speakeasies of various cities. You also got your vendor's pedaling refreshments and warm fried wraps. There's also a table to purchase pictures of your favorite vixen or IG models in next to nothing. Its crazy how the majority of us grew up trading sports cards to ending up in the FEDS trading these pictures of models like we did the Ken Griffey Jr and Michael Jordan cards. Times definitely have changed. If that's not your thing the indoor basketball courts showcase enough talent that you can possibly tap into the atmosphere of Harlem's own Holcombe Rucker Park. It's a great time killer. The best part of the whole outside rec area is the barbershop. Its attached to the area, so at any moment you can stop in for a fresh cut. Were all aware of the power of a fresh cut. When you look good you feel good. At that moment whatever it is that you're doing, your gonna do it good ten times out of ten, not nine. Plus, the barbershop captures the essence of the shop around the way. Sports talk, institution gossip and comic relief by some of the funniest characters to grace the compound. All of that while the backdrop ushers in the latest and hottest records from some of your favorite artist. It becomes another outlet to escape somewhat. Even if that scene is a little to loud for you and your more laidback artisan qualities, there is a painting room where you can discover your inner Basquiat or Andy Warhol.

"a couple items I got made in the ceramic department to celebrate my lady"

Some of the pieces the guys shell out at the prison belong in one of those stuffy pretentious art galleries. The talent is that impressive, at least once a week I would pop in at the paint shop to treat my eyes to the culture that was bouncing off each canvas.

There was also a ceramic room that would rival the china in your grandmother's china cabinets. These guys would master the trade, these ceramic creations were good enough to be sold at Williams Sonoma's or Pier One, some of the favorite retailers of housewives across America. This room would also serve as a time killer as well. I would comb the shelves with my eyes admiring the finished product for a decent amount of time. Across the hall there's a leather room with guys having the skill settings to assist any knock off organization, in creating replicas of high end handbags like a Chanel or Birkin bag. I even witnessed handbags made with ostrich skin. It would have been a perfect sweatshop to exploit for good quality and low wages.

Down another hall a newly opened room served as a game room

with a ping pong table. A fool's ball table and a four -man hockey

game where you spin the miniature hockey players to score a

goal. The game was a hit amongst the guys who frequented the

room. The room was a mini boys and girls club minus the girls,

and if you grew up in the boys and girls club of America

especially in the low income neighborhoods we came from, then

you know where I'm going with this. Within its first three days

of opening, a bar room type of brawl exploded in the room. After

surveying the damage, you could literally see the shape of each

torso that crashed through the dry wall of the room. The powers

that be eventually shut the room down for renovations and a

new approach for reopening the room. Security cameras that

solved everything. The room was back in full swing. I was

pleasantly surprised to find out the chapel wasn't only a place of

worship.

"Lil bro and I at the recreation area"

There was a room with 6 TV's and DVD players connected to them. With shelves of faith -based movies, they considered Star Wars a faith- based movie. So, you can imagine the classic's that hailed from the movie room. I would bring my turntable type headphones to bring AMC theater quality to my ears, with a bag full of snacks that would rival any movie theaters concession stand.

I also brought a thick scarf to rest my head on each side of my shoulder in cotton comfort. Since a kid I was always a movie buff. You could view me as the third wheel in the Siskel and Ebert duo who would critique movies. I found a slice of comfort. You would've thought I was a devout Christian the way I pulled open the doors of the chapel. That was just me securing a seat at the movies so to speak. That's no slight on the soul soothing religious teachings the building is known for. I sometimes skip the movie room to soak in the good word myself. I kind of put my foot in my mouth by revealing the escape the movie room could lend us prisoner's at times. Before I could look up the movie room would no longer have any empty seat in sight. I couldn't afford to lose out on my sanctuary. This was my peace of mind time. So, before I left my cell in route to the compound movie theater, I made sure to bring compound currency just in case every seat was taken, that was a sure way to levitate a likely candidate away from the controls of a movie station. It was worth the trade off every time. I always found my way over to the institution library. This was my natural habitat, a home away from home so to speak. Plus, the law library was in the same vicinity of the library. I needed to become well equipped with the Lexis Nexis law application to further my legal ambitions. So, I took a crash course on everything on how to learn the law application so I could be fully prepped and in the know when I enlist my next legal eagle. Screen time on the law library computer would turn me into a narcoleptic in no time or a heroin addict the way I kept nodding off.

I stood the course, before I forget to mention the biggest eye opener for me is when I first arrived to my assigned prison cell. As I met my cellmate I attempted to cast a light on my twenty-two -year sentence before my celly revealed to me that he was twenty years in already on a two hundred and thirteen -year prison sentence. The government sentenced this man as if he was one of those biblical figures I mentioned earlier with a few hundred years of life to live. My friend didn't even kill anybody or even attempt to. His sentence was draconian at best. That's a very wide lens into the henchman mentality sponsored by the American justice system. Despite my cellmates uphill battle his head never hung low. Instead he rose as a beacon of hope for the other guys on the compound. He lobbied single handedly for programs that would empower a large portion of inmates at the prison. He was the reason why guys were walking out of prison as certified personal trainers. I witnessed guys under his mentorship emerge as business owners when they got home. Proud owners of box gyms making an honest living. My friend Adam was reforming lives before my eyes. Much respect to the Adams of each prison. Within time I found my way around the law library. I was now surrounded by legal giants. It would be a meeting between the minds daily. My 2255 motion to vacate, set aside, or correct my sentence was taking shape and looking promising. Great men were instrumental into helping me author my arguments for my 2255. A few tweaks and I was ready to submit my motion to the courts. In the mean time I had a strong desire to uproot myself from the typical restraints prison can have on you. Instead of becoming a dust bunny getting sucked into the vacuum of the bullshit called prison politics as we know it. I was thinking more along the lines of emerging as a weapon of change. That weapon would be in the form of my first book my life story. A Memoir, I figured we all have a story to tell. I know the honesty of my story is enough to wake up at risk youth. Even if my story managed to alter one person's life that would be worth the project. I was now attempting to put my author's hat on. The idea of my story possibly triggering change in some was more than enough to rally my inner James Baldwin so to speak. Every chance I got I was putting pen to paper. I made a great investment and bought a mini lamp from commissary. Twenty-four hours in a day couldn't manage my newfound energy. You would catch me boxed in on the bottom bunk with my sheet cascading over my bunk, creating a makeshift wall in a dark room with my mini lamp illuminating my sheet of paper at three in the morning. I bet each paper I filled and ripped off its binder or each paper I crumbled and shot off towards the waste basket like a Steph Curry three pointer would launch my celly into a sleepless night. He never eluded to my noisy writing antic's. I guess he understood my determination to get this project up and running. I was the worst in the sense of being in mid conversation with someone and pulling out a fresh page I just finished. "let me know what you think about this?" Me being annoying. I noticed sharing each page with others and the feedback would prove a working remedy to see this project through. I knew a bunch of guys who were writing books themselves but eventually stalled out midway. Maybe they kept the project to themselves not knowing the power of feed back would be the fuel that would send them to the finish line. It's no different from a studio rapper or singer sharing a song with their entourage before releasing it. The feedback is critical. It was also encouraging that good vibes surrounded me in the most unlikely places. One early morning I was at the movie room sifting through a catalogue of movies when I over heard two guys discussing the cover art of a book one of the guys were holding. The guy holding the book said he had to get some things changed with his publisher. That was my cue to chime in, "You self- published that book?" My ear hustling put me in the right position. I walked away from that encounter with a bridge to properly self-publish my book with a new zest for writing. I wasted no time at reaching out to this haven of a publishing company that was assisting inmates in packaging their writing into book form from prison. Even getting us a spot on the digital book shelves of Amazon and Barnes and Nobles. All of this appeal was pulling me further into the pages of my life story. I was locked in and developing a callous on my writing hands middle finger on the side making writing difficult at times. The tools I used for writing were as primitive as what the Great

Shakespeare used to write Romeo and Juliet, a pen and paper. I'm sure he had the more polished writing utensil with the feather at the end. But who was I to complain. I even managed to get my cover art of my memoir graphically designed and digitalized for format. I kept a copy of my soon to be cover on me at all times. I was becoming an author before my very eyes. The feeling was intoxicating. I eventually got word from my inhouse legal eagle that my 2255 motion was ready to be sealed and mailed out. I did a careful review and exchanged a thumbs up with my chosen proxy. As soon as I dropped my legal mail in the mailbox, I felt a sort of relief like a boulder was removed from my shoulders. It felt right, now the waiting game would ensue. I met guys who were waiting for a response from the courts after three years. The way my inhouse legal team would advise me made me feel comfortable about the process. We were supplementing any new case law to the courts that spoke to my issues that were highlighted in my 2255. I felt like I had OJ Simpson's legal dream team, minus the murder case the way these bright minds would pull me over in the flow of inmate traffic. To tell me to meet them at the library so we can supplement new case law to my pending 2255 motion. A new promising case law dropped in 2019, Garza vs Idaho. My vehicle to get back in the courts was the ineffective assistance route. It was clear my attorney fell below the standard of sound counsel and this Garza case would be just what I needed to further my legal agenda. Meanwhile, I was warming up to the usual mold of prison life and landed a job in the medical department as an orderly. My job was to keep things squeaky clean and the floors buffed to a candy apple shimmer. I didn't mind the job, it broke up the monotony of the prison yard. I couldn't quite warm up to the blood spill portion of the job. This was the dark side of the gig. When someone was stabbed with a makeshift knife or when someone got their skull kicked in or even when someone was Mike Tysoned on the nose turning on the bloody faucet so to speak. I was the guy they called to clean up any blood spill. It didn't matter what time it was, whether one or two in the morning they were waking me up to disinfect the bloody scene. Yup! A violent feud between two cellmates explode at those hours as well. I was the guy walking up to the scene with a red bucket wrapped in cellophane. The red bucket consisted of a spray bottle to disinfect, a pair of gloves and a hazmat uniform if the scene was a bloody massacre. A red hazardous bag for bloody garments and a few packets of alcohol wipes. I was like the cleanup crew from a John Wick movie collecting my coin. That's right, every blood spill I showed up to would be a bonus into my inmate payroll. It's kind of crazy now that I think about it, how any violence involving blood was a bank deposit into my inmate account. When that type of violence kicked off every single inmate paid for it. The powers that be would shut down any movement for up to two weeks. If it was summertime we were practically being cooked inside our cells. The institution I was at was without any central air. That was just my type of luck! Those lockdowns kept my pulse on each pen I used to scribble my story to life. I was closing in on the last pages of my memoir. I named the book "I never claimed to have wings on" An Ex Drug Dealers cautionary tale, A memoir. I chose the title from a Hova line. It spoke to the message I was trying to convey in a clever way. Instead of sitting in my cell twiddling my thumbs, I decided I wanted to be more and do more. I wanted to inspire change from my prison cell. I was the same guy riddled with a drug dealer's false ambition. If I can get one kid to step away from trying to make money off selling drugs then my book is deemed a success. The book could even transition me into speaking engagements at the Boys and Girls Club or even juvenile placements. I owe that type of advocacy to my community. Remember how I said the FEDS are a nationwide operation, let me correct that, it's a worldwide fishing net that they cast out collecting folks from all corners of the world. With that being said, I couldn't understand how this federal prison was turning visitors away who were traveling from States away. Even worse, from countries away. I met a guy from Colombia a real humble person that never caused any trouble at the prison. Despite his family still living in Colombia their love for him was unshakable. So his family set up a visit. A flight from Colombia to Miami was charted and then a plane from Miami to the final stop in Erie, Pennsylvania. Hotel reservations had been made and a car rental to make the drive to the prison. The traveling alone amounts to a pretty penny. The visit was scheduled for Saturday and Sunday. My friend's daughter who he hasn't seen in years joined the convoy of family coming to see him. His excitement levels were through the roof. I was extremely happy for him. Friday morning comes rolling in and a royal rumble of a fight breaks out in the chow hall at breakfast. The powers that be shut the prison down as far as inmate movements go. The lockdown spills into Saturday and the worst is yet to come. Visitation for the compound was cancelled for the weekend. My friend's spirit was destroyed and more so for his family arriving all the way from South America. They figure shut it down which means less work for them, not knowing these inconsiderate decisions tear families further apart. Family support is a key driving force to usher in change in one's life. Some of these federal institutions are making visitation privileges a tall task for our families. There not mindful of the wear and tear these trips have on our loved ones, than to just turn around and deny access to your family for bogus reasons. With all due respect to my dear friend, but I know a guy personally that was serving time with me that tragically lost his family a few miles away from the prison in a car accident. God rest their souls. These institutions that designate inmates to these far away prisons need to reassess how guys are being sent to prisons that are obscene hours away, even states away. The toll and danger fall's on the family. The crazy part is these institutions supposedly encourage family support on paper, but in reality their only discouraging families from keeping in contact with their incarcerated family. The worst part is these prison factory's rather prisoners be without support so the inmate can tunnel further into the pipeline they constructed. They know a lack of support is a key ingredient to poison the prisoner further. It's like rehabilitation disrupts their bottom line. Our incarceration creates generational wealth for these wicked oligarchies. My eyes were wide open to the bullshit agenda reverberating through the prisons of America. Through it all, I remained focus and on course. My books manuscript was ready to be turned over to my self publishing team. I was feeling accomplished that I managed to finish something positive that I started. There was enough distractions at the prison to divide me from my goals. Not caving empowered me. The day I mailed out my manuscript, I received a response from the government concerning my 2255 motion. A response served as a formality. Naturally the government opposes any arguments made by the pro se movant. My inhouse legal eagle and I responded back to the government. Now it would be up to my district judge to give his final say concerning my motion. It's I either get denied for lacking merit or my motion gets granted for showing merit in each of my claims detailed in my motion. With my 2255 pending the ball was rolling so to speak. With President Trump signing off on the historical First Step Act this would be the biggest reform federal inmates seen in a very long time. Guys were benefiting greatly with this. The First Step Act was slicing prison terms in half. I was watching guys get early release left and right. It was most rewarding when a guy was standing by on the unit waiting for a recreation move with his gym bag hanging off his neck with a look of "Here we go again, a day in the life of prison" to only get his thoughts interrupted by the unit manager or counselor telling the guy to pack his belongings he is going home. The gravity of that type of surprise was enormous, to think you were headed to the prison yard to work out and instead you pivot into a surprise release. There was a domino effect of prisoners getting back in court for relief. The prison population suddenly felt hopeful. I remember an old timer named L.A from my home state with a life sentence. He used to always remind me "Don't even worry champ, we both getting out soon" I used to admire his hope. He was already twenty plus years in on his life sentence. A few weeks went by and my friend L.A was headed to court and was finally released. I was beyond happy for him. His high spirit and hopeful energy will always remain with me. I believed something good was coming my way. I remember I used to go up to guys who were being released and shake their hand while telling them "I'm just trying to tap into the electrical energy of what freedom feels like" with a wide smile. Seeing guys get time back in droves reinvigorated my spirit. Trump was being hailed as some sort of hero in the federal prison for his handling of the First Step Act. Guys would joke and say Trump signed off on the new law because of how he and his cohorts would straddle the fine line of shady living. Maybe the new law would serve as a potential life line in the event of the collapse of the Trump outfit. Either way, the First Step Act would be a remedy in the right direction for us prisoners of war. However, there's a whole lot of work to be done. It's mind boggling to know people are serving life sentences for non- violent drug offenses. I know of guys with marijuana charges serving out their natural life in federal custody. How is that just? When you now have legal marijuana syndicates on all corners of America being praised for inflating the economy. While my fellow comrades who were in the same business are serving lengthy prison terms or even given life sentences. The hypocrisy is alive. Again, my eyes were open to the clandestine agenda being administered on us marginalized people by the fat cats. I was floored to receive my manuscript in book form one afternoon during mail call. Just to see my book come alive was the most fulfilling. The fact that I managed to create the book from my prison cell was a win for myself and others. What you don't reveal you can't heal. I can honestly say the healing process did wonders for me. Now my story can be used as that weapon of change for our -at- risk youth. To know that my book is now available on Amazon and Barnes and Nobles online is still crazy to me. *I never claimed to have wings on, an ex-drug dealer's cautionary tale.* Again, how surreal. I wasn't going to allow prison to dim my lights and through the grace of god and my in-house legal eagles, A twinkle at the end of the tunnel was suddenly illuminating in the form of my 2255 motion after eighteen months. On the seventh day of October 2019 and evidentiary hearing is granted on my claims that my counsel was ineffective. I was headed back to court. My claims held merit and I was finally going to be heard. I was erupting with pure joy. My book was now available to the masses and I had a new day in court. On the tenth day of March 2020 I was summoned to show up to federal court. I was ecstatic to say the least. With my motion being granted the courts appointed me a new attorney Pro bono. That last bit of information would release the feel good butterflies fluttering in the pit of my stomach. I felt like I was being encased in relief despite not knowing what type of reduction in my prison sentence I would stand to benefit. Just to get back to the courtroom is a win. This would be my chance to articulate to the courts that my prior counsel hindered each step of my procedural process. The guy botched my due process plain and simple. My new attorney was also granted a chance to amend his professional legal touch regarding my ineffective assistance claims. When he sent me his version of arguments in lieu of my position my inhouse legal team and I felt like the approach was too thin to win so to speak. Regardless our formula is what got me back in court so I kind of dismissed his legal advice until I was able to get a face to face with him. Unfortunately that meeting never happened in the three and a half months he was assigned to my case he never showed up to the prison to go over strategy with me. We had one unprofessional legal call that didn't sit well with me. Before you know it, I was packed up on the prison bus in route to United States Penitentiary Canaan for transit purposes. This go around wouldn't be a four -hour layover. Instead the prison would host me for a week of absolute darkness. No phone calls, No Corrlinks to message my folks, limited showers, and the barest one can be concerning food and hygiene products. Maybe an hour out your cell a day. It's a tall glass to swallow, but for a new day in court I'm chugging away with ease. I now meet people who were just like me in transit heading to their designated prison. Without even realizing it I became the voice of reason for the new guys coming through with a disparity of a sentence. Something I knew all too well about. Despite the odds drowning some in despair my energy and latest victory in landing a court date would serve as a life jacket. Keeping guys afloat. Instilling a form of hope. After a week of sampling the cold and cruel transit ward of USP Canaan I was awakened at 3a.m by a correctional guard and chaperoned to the prison bus for some diesel therapy. My next stop would be Harrisburg International airport in Pennsylvania. Guys who never boarded an airplane due to fear of flying were now facing their fear head on. If you ever seen the movie Conair starring Nicholas Cage than maybe that can give you a much better visual of what was unfolding before my eyes. Lucky for me I wasn't boarding any flight. Instead my window seat on the bus exposed me to armed flight attendants guiding my fellow convicts on the airplane as opposed to your tight skirt wearing bubbly stewardess. The portion of the tarmac we occupied unveiled armed U.S Marshalls cradling the M16 military weapon menacingly itching to send a flurry of finger sized bullets in the direction of any escape plot. Woman prisoners were also being boarded on the BOP's version of Conair sending my fellow bus passengers into a frenzy. Meanwhile, I was in complete discomfort with the way the handcuffs dug into my wrist and ankles along with a dog chain that squeezed my diaphragm like a waist trainer. I could no longer focus on the eye jarring scene taking place outside my window seat. Eventually the engine would roar back to life creating an eye sore along the highways of Pennsylvania. I would look out my window peeking into the vehicle traveling along this mad max type of prison bus I was on, locking eyes with the driver or backseat passenger until one of us looked away in embarrassment. I would space out for some time letting the weight of what I was going through weigh me down mentally. Than the news feed amongst inmates would steal my attention. Some guys were giving their best Nostradamus predictions regarding where the bus will make its next lay over location. The thought was MDC Brooklyn for a week than FDC Philly until court. I naturally envisioned MDC Brooklyn due to the route the prison bus made when I first came through the federal system, but to my surprise we ended up at FDC Philly. To learn that I didn't have to spend a week or so in Brooklyn before my Philly stop was rewarding. To my delight I was housed on five south which was the same unit I once departed from on route to the federal pipeline. Some of the same guys I left behind were still on the unit. I would stand to benefit the essentials like shower shoes to protect my feet from falling off. Commissary in the form of food and hygiene products. I was also given a radio to tune into the five TV's on the unit, but most importantly the guys who I left behind were excited that I was back in the building due to my 2255 motion being granted. My small victory would spell out hope for the fellas. I laid out some valuable insight regarding new supreme court rulings that could provide some fire power in their defense. Then I wasted no time at revealing that I wrote a book and got it published which is now available on Amazon and Barnes and Nobles. One of the guys I was telling this to secretly slid off and called his folks on the outside to fact check if I really had a book out. He walked up to me and congratulated me for the feat. He also had a copy sent in for him that he asked me to sign. This was a new feeling and it sure felt good. I eventually spun my small stint back in the building as a full -blown book tour. I promoted my book to everybody and anybody. When a guy's book would show up during mail call they made sure to hold it up in the air if I was across the unit or on the phone. I bet the feeling was equivalent to an artist hearing his song on the radio for the first time. It was a huge rush to say the least. I then bumped into another guy from Allentown who was in the building to get time back due to the benefits of the highly anticipated First Step Act. He did all his time in the penitentiary crashing out in volatile acts of aggression for the better half of his time. He knew that type of prison record would cast a bad light on his chances of getting the max time off his remaining prison sentence. Either way he was getting time back. It was the last week of February 2020 and my court date was scheduled for March 10,2020. I was wondering if I was going to court from Philly or if I was going to get sent to my county prison in Allentown. I was scheduled for federal court in Easton, Pennsylvania which is twenty minutes away from Allentown. I'm still not sure why I was issued a federal judge out there when Allentown has its own federal courthouse. I guess everything about the FEDS are complicated by design. Then the thing I feared most during these transit locations happened, all of my legal documents pertaining to prep me for my court hearing was supposedly lost in the shuffle of transferring to each prison. I was beyond furious. These were key documents that would prepare me mentally to spar verbally in legal jargon at my evidentiary hearing. Every authority figure in Philly who had some type of stature would fail me in locating my arsenal of legal work. To make matter's worse my court appointed attorney never showed up to Philly to show how invested he was in my case. The red flags were showing up in every direction that the gears in my head were spinning. To my surprise and pleasure Lehigh County Prison came to pick me up to bring me back to Allentown. I was excited about the trip just to be able to lay eyes on the city once again would do wonders for my spirit. I arrived at the county prison on March 3 and three days later I made it to the inmate population on 2D of the prison. As soon as I stepped onto the unit I recognized a few guys who swiftly made sure some sort of comfort reached me in the form of commissary. Than a close friend popped out the woodwork with a copy of my book that I published. I felt like my song was playing on the radio again so to speak. My hard work was now generating legal funds for the first time in my life. The fact that I was able to complete a book project while serving a twenty plus year prison sentence loomed over me and reminded me of my strength. Being in the county prison because of my own relentless will to bury myself in the law library to furnish some just results was a confidence booster for me. Naturally the guys who knew me somewhat or heard of me would give me a peculiar stare or vibe because I was back from Federal Prison after being sentenced to a term of twenty-two years behind bars. Federal drug cases usually garner so called press in the community we hail from. The rumor mill will take on a life of its own, even with a twenty- two- year prison sentence I heard guys on the streets kicking my back in so to speak. Even if I would of got a life sentence I bet there would of been people speculating, "why didn't he get the death penalty? something is off about that" or if I got the death penalty they would probably say, "I'm surprised they didn't kill him on the spot". Even though my case didn't warrant any of those disparities. It was the nature of people working the underbelly of society. I wouldn't fault them, they just didn't know any better. It was March 9,2020 a day before my court date and guess who decides to finally drop in? My court appointed attorney. He figured it would be convenient to cram in all his questions and strategy the day before my court hearing. I knew this song and dance all to well. There was no way I was going to allow this ill-advised man to represent me in the biggest fight of my life. I was fooled once by my first counsel and I wouldn't travel down memory lane with this pretender. After my meeting with my counsel I arranged a phone call to the law offices of Allentown's own John Waldron a reputable and dependable attorney. I passed along that I was firing my attorney and that I had a court hearing scheduled for tomorrow and that I need him to ask the judge for a continuance. Being that I wanted to change attorney's last minute, I would have to go to my court date and articulate to the judge of my decision of releasing my assigned counsel of his duties , because I was going with a hired attorney. When I arrived at court I told my counsel that I was going in another direction with my own attorney. He turned beet red, I could tell he felt undermined. Either way I wasn't there to gauge his feelings. The judge was quickly brought up to speed. I don't think he was to fond of the new developments unraveling in his courtroom. I believe his mind set was to chip away at his scheduled court hearings for the day. Then again, I wasn't rushing this life altering hearing for nobody or allowing for a below standard counsel who could care less if I triumph or not to represent me any longer. I would like to think the judge understood the gravity of my qualms and granted me the continuance to establish my private attorney. I also requested if I could remain in the county prison due to how far I would be from my new attorney and how my prior lawyers never let me be a part of each step of my due process. I was so relieved that the request was granted to me. When I got back to the county prison I reached for a commissary sheet and immediately purchased a TV and other items to try my hand at getting cozy for the time being. Having a TV in my cell was a lost luxury federally. I was taking full advantage and finally catching up to pop culture along with my front row seat at the movies so to speak. A visit every three days with my lady behind the glass wasn't too shabby. Plus, the prison is a towering building in the center of the city. I was always climbing on the seat attached to my cells desk looking out the window with the focus of a peeping Tom, but instead of being creepy like Tom I was sizing up the landscape of the city that grew me. Despite being boxed in, it felt good to be as close as I was to the gridiron I once took snaps on. However, I was fully reformed from that lifestyle wholeheartedly. The guys who were just passing through the prison especially the younger guys with the drug dealers twinkle illuminating from their eyes, I would share my experience's and a copy of my book in hopes to quiet the destructive tides building up in them. I forgot how restricted the county was. We were always in the cell and this is when the TV would prove its worth. I was the worst TV operator, a total serial channel surfer. I watched three programs at a time flickering back and forth. I would hear my cellmate kiss his teeth out of frustration with me or rather roll over in his bunk facing the wall out of protest of the abuse I shelled out with all my remote controlling. This wasn't me going out of my way to be a dickhead, its just that I wanted to watch everything all at once. I started to notice all of this coverage from the powerhouse news outlets like CNN, MSNBC, and FOX news about a virus called Coronavirus which also goes by COVID-19. I didn't really pay it no mind until prison officials made an announcement that visits were suspended until further notice. Our lawyers were even prohibited from visiting. They even sliced our recreation time in half, court dates were adjourned until further notice. The environment turned high strung when the guards passed out cloth face mask to each inmate. The news reported an alarming death toll that was surging out of control. This pandemic wasn't only a United States issue this virus was a worldwide pandemic of biblical proportion, apocalyptic in nature. We were all afraid for our families. Eventually the county ushered in Ipad like tablets with the Facetime option. This was the new norm as they say in county prison which wasn't to bad. I was able to stay in tune with up to date movies, I also had an account with iheart radio allowing for me to have access to new music while still enjoying classic records. Aside from Facetime I would get lost for hours on the cult classic game of Pac-Man. I had to give the county credit for allowing these amenities to comfort me somewhat. I would also go on another book tour so to speak. I would have miniature flyers of my book cover sent in to promote on the unit. Guys were showing support and ordering my book in droves from the good folks over at Amazon.

It was shocking when the States went on full blown lock down. This Covid-19 was decimating the fabric of life as we know it. The fact that people of color were affected at a higher rate wasn't even surprising to me. The institutions that run the world wouldn't have it any other way. The disparities were fanning the flames of other things to come. On May 30, 2020 I was in my cell channel surfing like I normally do when I came across news coverage regarding the heinous murder of a black man named George Floyd. He was killed by a Minneapolis Police officer. People of color being killed by cops was nothing new but with cell phone cameras being the phenomenon this callous modern day lynching was captured in its entirety. Within a few hours I was watching the city of Minneapolis ignite in flames and chaos. It looked like a scene out of the Watts riot deriving from the infamous beat down that Rodney King endured by the L.A.P.D. However, the comparison was way off. Every city in the United States of America erupted in flames and destruction in protest for George Floyd. Excuse the understatement, there were actually protest erupting all over the world in unity for justice for George Floyd. The unrest even reached the county prison I was in. It was like a scene out of the movie Lean on me starring Morgan Freeman where protester's chanted outside the prison "Free Mr. Clark" but instead the large mass of protesters chanting "Black Lives Matter" with bullhorns and posters spelling out "Justice or no peace" young people were leading the charge. It was historical to say the least. It felt like I had a front row seat into the destructive path the Coronavirus was blazing or joining the legion of protesters swarming the streets of America through my TV set. These were uncertain times. I was getting news that Federal prisons were on complete lockdown due to the Coronavirus and the civil unrest breaking out in America. I was sort of blessed to be on Federal writ at my county prison during these tumultuous times. Even though there was no court date in sight I felt good about my chances down the road. The needle was already moving in my favor so to speak. But I would be remiss if I was to say my positive attitude alone kept me upright and head high through my ongoing journey through the Federal inferno of prison. That my fight was solely me and my inhouse legal eagles. Nope! They say behind every successful man there's a great woman. In my case, behind every positive stride I made there was a phenomenal woman. My lovely fiancée Anna. Rarely do we spotlight our significant other in the shadow's doing hard time with us. Most of the genuine love they envelope us with goes unnoticed and not because were spiteful but sometimes the plight we are facing consumes us. All we see is the bullshit raining down on us, but what about them? Or how they worry about us. How our issues serve them like a strong cup of caffeine keeping our women frazzled by sleepless nights. What about the long driving expeditions or the connecting flights they board just to come see us. How the invasion of privacy they endure when being screened by the prison's version of the infamous TSA for visitation access. Or how they pick up the phone on the first ring when we call, how they know the food rations amount to a child's portion size and how slop is the main course, so they help you in that disparity by keeping you stocked with commissary. How they figure out the right words to put you at ease when the stress is unbearable. I give a standing ovation to my rock Anna and all the strong woman holding their men up through the hardship of incarceration. We see you and we applaud your superwoman powers. The prison pipeline is a nasty business affecting your loved ones just as much as you. You rode the school bus to prison through these pages with me. Hopefully it was big enough window to give you a valid look into how the two institutions of School and prison deceive you according to your zip code. Stay Woke! To be continued.

"my fiancée and I lending each other some warmth at a visit"

"After five hours of tedious driving she still managed to smile. She's one of one"

ABOUT THE AUTHOR

John Raymond Melendez Jr. was sentenced to 262 months in Federal prison. He currently resides in Federal custody where he continues to write and litigate to get his fair chance in court to finally do better in society than a warehouse of a prison. Jrmelpublishing@gmail.com

Photo Credits

Prosthetic Leg- Courtesy of Hope to Walk

Wired Mouth- Courtesy of Exodontia.info

Prison Boot Camp- Courtesy of Alamy

Prison Cell- Courtesy of MSN.Com

Sneakers- Courtesy of Sole Collector

Printed in Great Britain
by Amazon

50278246R00098